HOLLY'S
PICTURESQUE
COUNTRY SEATS

HOLLY'S PICTURESQUE COUNTRY SEATS

A Complete Reprint of the 1863 Classic

HENRY HUDSON HOLLY

With a New Introduction by
George B. Tatum

DOVER PUBLICATIONS, INC.
NEW YORK

TO

The American Institute of Architects,

———•••———

Copyright

Introduction copyright © 1993 by George B. Tatum.
All rights reserved under Pan American and International Copyright Conventions.

Published in Canada by General Publishing Company, Ltd., 30 Lesmill Road, Don Mills, Toronto, Ontario.
Published in the United Kingdom by Constable and Company, Ltd., 3 The Lanchesters, 162–164 Fulham Palace Road, London W6 9ER.

Bibliographical Note

This Dover edition, first published in 1993, is an unabridged republication of *Holly's Country Seats: Containing Lithographic Designs for Cottages, Villas, Mansions, etc., with Their Accompanying Outbuildings; also, Country Churches, City Buildings, Railway Stations, etc., etc.,* originally published by D. Appleton and Company, New York, in 1863. A new introduction has been written specially for this edition by George B. Tatum.

Library of Congress Cataloging-in-Publication Data

Holly, Henry Hudson, 1834–1892.
    [Holly's country seats]
    Holly's picturesque country seats : a complete reprint of the 1863 classic / Henry Hudson Holly ; with a new introduction by George B. Tatum.
        p.   cm.
    Originally published: Holly's country seats. New York : D. Appleton, 1863.
    Includes bibliographical references.
    ISBN 0-486-27856-5
    1. Architecture, Domestic—United States—Designs and plans. 2. Architecture, English—Influence. I. Title.
NA7205.H63 1993
720'.92—dc20
                                         93-6164
                                           CIP

Manufactured in the United States of America
Dover Publications, Inc., 31 East 2nd Street, Mineola, N.Y. 11501

HOLLY'S PICTURESQUE COUNTRY SEATS

A Complete Reprint of the 1863 Classic

HENRY HUDSON HOLLY

With a New Introduction by
George B. Tatum

DOVER PUBLICATIONS, INC.
NEW YORK

TO

The American Institute of Architects,

THIS BOOK IS

RESPECTFULLY DEDICATED,

BY

THE AUTHOR.

———•♦•———

Copyright

Introduction copyright © 1993 by George B. Tatum.
All rights reserved under Pan American and International Copyright Conventions.

Published in Canada by General Publishing Company, Ltd., 30 Lesmill Road, Don Mills, Toronto, Ontario.
Published in the United Kingdom by Constable and Company, Ltd., 3 The Lanchesters, 162–164 Fulham Palace Road, London W6 9ER.

Bibliographical Note

This Dover edition, first published in 1993, is an unabridged republication of *Holly's Country Seats: Containing Lithographic Designs for Cottages, Villas, Mansions, etc., with Their Accompanying Outbuildings; also, Country Churches, City Buildings, Railway Stations, etc., etc.,* originally published by D. Appleton and Company, New York, in 1863. A new introduction has been written specially for this edition by George B. Tatum.

Library of Congress Cataloging-in-Publication Data

Holly, Henry Hudson, 1834–1892.
    [Holly's country seats]
    Holly's picturesque country seats : a complete reprint of the 1863 classic / Henry Hudson Holly ; with a new introduction by George B. Tatum.
        p.   cm.
    Originally published: Holly's country seats. New York : D. Appleton, 1863.
    Includes bibliographical references.
    ISBN 0-486-27856-5
    1. Architecture, Domestic—United States—Designs and plans. 2. Architecture, English—Influence. I. Title.
NA7205.H63 1993
720'.92—dc20
                                    93-6164
                                        CIP

Manufactured in the United States of America
Dover Publications, Inc., 31 East 2nd Street, Mineola, N.Y. 11501

INTRODUCTION TO
THE DOVER EDITION

———•••———

DESPITE the interest of some of his commissions, the popularity of at least two of his three books and the high regard in which he was held by his professional contemporaries, Henry Hudson Holly (1834–1892) has remained a somewhat shadowy figure in the annals of American architecture. Modern surveys of the subject mention him only in passing, if at all. And though he is accorded a brief—if not entirely accurate—paragraph in Henry and Elsie Withey's *Biographical Dictionary of American Architects*,[1] there is no entry for him in the four-volume *Macmillan Encyclopedia of Architects*, published as recently as 1982.

By his own account,[2] Holly was born and reared in New York City, the seventh of nine children of William Welles Holly, a prosperous merchant who dabbled in local politics successfully enough to be elected alderman.[3] That the Hollys were well-to-do has been inferred from the address and character of their residence, which was located on Fifth Avenue (then an unpaved road on the outskirts of the city) and set amid grounds that extended a full block to the west.[4]

Rather than following his father in a career in commerce or politics, when Holly was 20, he elected to study architecture. This was in 1854, three years before American architects succeeded in forming a viable professional organization and a decade before the Massachusetts Institute of Technology established the first architectural curriculum at a major American institution of higher learning.[5] Had he been born a few years later, Holly might well have followed the lead of Richard Morris Hunt in attending the École des Beaux-Arts in Paris, as did a number of his younger contemporaries.[6] As it was, he continued the long-established custom of preparing for a career in architecture by entering the office of a practicing architect. His choice of mentor was Gervase Wheeler,[7] an emigrant from England whose New York office was then in the Trinity Building at 111 Broadway, an address popular with others of his profession.

Wheeler was one of a number of English architects who had elected to immigrate to the United States during the 1840s and 1850s. Whereas even before the end of the eighteenth century American painters had begun to seek instruction in Continental cities, especially Paris,[8] prior to the Civil War American architects were usually content to follow the lead of England, particularly in matters related to designs for church and home. This explains why Andrew Jackson Downing (1815–1852), then the acknowledged American arbiter of taste, hired two British architects, Calvert Vaux (1824–1895) and Frederick Clarke Withers (1828–1901), as the two young assistants who would enable him to establish a practice of his own.[9] Nor must it have seemed in any way inappropriate that Richard Upjohn (1802–1878), a man born and trained in Dorset County, England, became the founder and first president of the American Institute of Architects.

On his arrival in the United States sometime during the 1840s, Wheeler first settled in Connecticut.[10] There he may have become acquainted with the Holly family, which had long had close ties to the city of Stamford, where for a time Holly would continue to reside even after opening his own architectural office in nearby New York City. While practicing in Connecticut, Wheeler sent a design for a "Villa in the Tudor Style" to *The Horticulturist*, the monthly "Journal of Rural Art and Rural Taste" that Downing had been editing since its introduction by Luther Tucker, the Albany publisher, some three years earlier.

Wheeler's design, which appeared in *The Horticulturist* for June 1849, could fairly be criticized for attempting to combine architectural elements from too many historical periods. Presumably it satisfied Downing, however, for two months later he offered his readers another of Wheeler's house designs. This was a symmetrical "English Cottage" built of wood and similar to one Wheeler had designed for a client in Brunswick, Maine.[11] All things considered, Wheeler's English cottage must be considered an improvement over his earlier Tudor villa, and with due credit to its designer, Downing used it again as Figure 130 in his *Architecture of Country Houses*, published by D. Appleton and Company the following year.[12]

Perhaps encouraged by Downing's apparent acceptance of his work, Wheeler considered joining the growing number of American authors of books of house designs. He began, however, by publishing a series of articles in *The Home Journal*, beginning March 1, 1851 and signed simply "G. W." Aimed at "promoting comfort and fitness in a home," the pieces in *The Home Journal* were received well enough that later the same year Charles Scribner was willing to publish all of them together under the title *Rural Homes*. In these "sketches of houses suited to American country life," Wheeler's penchant for combining disparate architectural forms, noted earlier, is perhaps even more apparent. And although Downing does not mention this as a specific fault, in a long review in *The Horticulturist* for December 1, 1851, he takes Wheeler to task for badly misleading his readers. While admitting that the text of *Rural Homes* was "sprightly" and "readable" enough, Downing found its author another of those "pseudo-architects from abroad, who leave home with too small a smattering of professional knowledge to ensure success at home, and after three or four years of practice in this country . . . undertake to *direct* the popular taste . . . ." The ineptness of some of Wheeler's designs appears the more surprising when it is recalled that he trained in England under Richard Carpenter (1812–1855), a designer of recognized ability and one of the leading proponents of the use of Gothic for Anglican churches.

Downing's unfavorable opinion apparently did not affect the demand for *Rural Homes*; during the next twenty years, it was reprinted at least eight times. Nor did it prevent Wheeler from having his work published by the increasingly popular *Godey's Lady's Book*[13] or from bringing out still another book of house designs. By almost any standard, *Homes for the People in Suburb Country*, first published in 1855 and reprinted at least five times thereafter, represented a marked improvement over its author's first book.[14] Whether it might have led Downing to temper his earlier criticism we can only guess, for he had perished three years earlier in the burning of the Hudson River steamer *Henry Clay*. We do know, however, that a year after

Downing's death, *The Horticulturist* published Wheeler's design for a villa in the currently popular Italianate mode.[15] This was, in fact, one of the styles especially favored by Wheeler and used by him in about 1855 for the Rochester house of Patrick Barry, the nurseryman who for several years edited *The Horticulturist* as Downing's successor.[16]

Despite what appears to have been a growing acceptance of Wheeler's designs, Holly may have considered the training available to him in the United States insufficient. At least, the better part of 1856 he spent in Europe, where he could observe at firsthand the sources for much of American design. On his return to New York City later the same year, Holly opened his own office, briefly with Charles Duggin (1830-1916),[17] who had emigrated from London in 1853, and subsequently by himself at 335 Broadway. Holly's arrival on the architectural scene did not go unnoticed by his contemporaries. Shortly after his return from Europe, he was unanimously elected to membership in the newly formed American Institute of Architects.[18] This was a signal honor for one so young, and to show his appreciation, Holly later dedicated his first book to the Institute.

In order to bring his professional qualifications to the attention of the American public, early in his career Holly followed Wheeler's example by publishing a book of house designs. Titled *Country Seats* and aimed at the growing middle class, Holly's book was similar to those being produced by a majority of his most successful contemporaries. In an era when architecture was just emerging as a recognized profession, when there were no American periodicals devoted solely to the subject and when fees for design and superintendence had yet to be fully recognized, let alone standardized, such architectural books not only provided welcome income for their authors but were often an effective means for securing commissions. To be sure, most clients simply engaged local builders to adapt designs found in one or more books, without further reference to the author or authors. On occasion, however, the original designer might be paid to supply about a half-dozen drawings by mail; only rarely would he be engaged to visit the site or to supervise construction.

Unlike the earlier "builders' guides" that consisted largely of architectural details principally of use to craftsmen, the publications of Holly and other architects of his time were of the "pattern book" variety. These provided complete designs, viewed in perspective, usually in a landscape setting, and accompanied by a text explaining to the client and the builder the rationale for their adoption. The first American pattern book is usually considered to have been Alexander J. Davis' *Rural Residences,* which bears the date 1837, but which did not come out until 1838.[19] This was to have appeared serially, however, and because only the first two numbers were published, because of its relatively large format and because of the hand-colored lithographs that served as illustrations, *Rural Residences* cannot be said to have supplied the model for the many pattern books published during the following half-century. It remained for Downing to demonstrate the success of books of smaller size, bound by the publisher in cloth, and produced in fairly large editions at a comparatively modest price. Published initially during the 1840s, Downing's books were followed by similar works by Vaux, Withers, Upjohn—and of course Wheeler—as well as by numerous others. Throughout the nineteenth century, there were few years that did not see the publication of at least one or two architectural books, and in times of greatest prosperity, the number was nearer a dozen.[20]

Although its principal topic was landscape gardening, Downing's first book included a chapter on rural architecture, a subject to which its author devoted increased attention as his career progressed. Perhaps with Downing's example in mind, Holly noted in the preface to *Country Seats* that he, too, had originally intended to include a "Treatise on Landscape Gardening,"[21] in this case by George E. Waring, Jr. (1833–1898). Waring, a sanitary engineer then engaged in providing the elaborate drainage system for New York's Central Park, was unable to provide the treatise, however; when he accepted a commission in the Union Army, the plan was dropped.[22] For assistance with putting his designs on the lithographic stone, in the preface to *Country Seats* Holly also acknowledged his debt to Paul Schulze (1827–1897), a Prussian artist who had recently moved to New York City from Boston. At the time of his association with Holly, Schulze had already designed several buildings for Harvard College and with various partners would later receive important commissions in New York City and Washington, D.C.

In addition to depriving him of Waring's contribution, Holly tells us that the "War for the Union" also forced him to delay the publication of his first book until 1863, even though the manuscript for *Country Seats* had been completed some two years earlier. Indeed, the War and the many dislocations that attended it must have put an end to all but the most essential building throughout much of the United States.

Presumably it was this lack of commissions in wartime that led Wheeler to decide to return to England, thereby bringing to an end a career that spanned 20 years in his adopted country. Last listed as practicing in Brooklyn in 1860, by 1865 Wheeler was back in London. There, in 1868 he discussed the "Peculiarities of Domestic Architecture in America" before the Royal Institute of British Architects, of which he had been elected a Fellow the year before.[23] Wheeler's third and last book, *The Choice of a Dwelling*, was published (perhaps posthumously) in London in 1871. There appears to have been a second printing the following year, but if the author received any English commissions of importance, none are known. Nor apart from a few examples like the old chapel at Williams College (1857), the house for Henry Boody in Brunswick, Maine,[24] and that for Patrick Barry in Rochester, New York, do any of Wheeler's American buildings survive.

Following a common practice of the time, Holly devoted a good part of his first book—the opening 32 pages, in this case—to a wide-ranging history of his subject, a survey in which facts are freely combined with a generous measure of myth, conjecture and opinion. In the wake of the Second World War, courses in the history of art and architecture would become commonplace, television would acquaint Americans with cultures the world over, and a plethora of books on all aspects of the arts would be offered to the reading public at affordable prices. When Holly was writing, however, the modern concept of style as distinctive cultural expression was comparatively new and unfamiliar. Rather than appearing stale or hackneyed, the material presented in the opening section of *Country Seats* may well have impressed its first readers as novel, even exciting.[25] Predictably, Holly stresses the extent to which much American architecture was then derived from that of England and echoes the views of Downing and other writers of the period in praising English country life. The first section of *Country Seats* ends with a plea to cull from history those elements that should enable American architects to evolve a distinctive style, one that would compare favorably with that of any of the greatest nations of the past.

an villa we have come to expect in books of this kind, but many of
have lost the national or stylistic identification common in
s. Instead, Holly's readers are offered simply "A Square Stone
Irregular House with a Veranda all Round" or simply a
a Village Lot." This practice may also be found in other pattern
authors, too, appear to be seeking a distinctly American style
any specific foreign model. To that end, Holly continues—albeit
greater degree—Downing's emphasis on overhanging roofs,
brackets,[29] clustered chimneys, an assortment of bays and oriels
se, the ubiquitous veranda. And much as Downing had before
ral instances Holly illustrates how, by the judicious addition of
es as these, a plain square or rectangular house might be
regular, and thereby picturesque.

ion with other designs of the period, Holly's betray their mid-
late by their greater verticality and by an overall lightness of
latter characteristic he achieved in part by exposing portions of
on the exterior, where slender wooden members and diagonal
ction as a distinguishing part of the design. So far as American
e is concerned, the origins of this practice have been traced at
back as Downing and through him to a number of his successors
rs. Thus Wheeler, noting the ready availability of wood through-
f the United States, sought to make a virtue of necessity by
y designing structures that relied for their effect on their wooden
al or apparent.[30] Since in cases of this kind the resultant
was likely to be of so many wooden sticks, historians conveniently
as the "Stick Style."[31]

ound many of the qualities he was seeking in a distinctly
architecture expressed in the writing of Charles Lock Eastlake
6), the son of the English painter Sir Charles Eastlake and himself
ul designer of furnishings and interiors. Though well received
published in London in 1868, Eastlake's *Hints on Household Taste*
ps even more popular in the United States, where there were
ions or reprintings between 1872 and 1883.

unately, Holly was so pleased with Eastlake's ideas that he
to credit their originator when he borrowed freely from them for a

A second and last printing of *Country* .
years after the first had appeared. That
doubtless had much to do with inevitable
waning enthusiasm for the picturesque c
and Davis had introduced a generation ea
tive Schulze's illustrations as works of art,
readily lend itself to the clear detail desire
wood engravings found in most house pat
while, Holly's personal life was changing. C
his own book, or shortly thereafter, he ma
mother, under the name "Aunt Fanny," v
children's stories. Sarah, too, had written a
practice to which she returned in later life.

Although *Country Seats* focuses prima
Holly also offered his readers a design for a
for churches.[27] The latter are good exampl
produced originally in medieval England
nineteenth century, especially by those i
revival that had started in England and spre
in fact, no coincidence that during this pe
American pattern books dealing specifically
the work of men trained in England, notably
Clarke Withers.[28] Holly, for his part, was
smaller of the two churches featured in *Cou*
had designed for Wilton, Connecticut, and in
series of some 35 "original" designs under t
tecture. Apparently this undertaking met
however; surviving copies are comparatively
printings were called for and its author contin
a designer of domestic structures.

Even when identified with the name of anc
residential designs are still clearly based c
occasionally, as in the case of the prominent m
is there a hint of America's growing enthusia
pages of *Country Seats* we meet again the Swis

and the Ital
the design:
earlier boo
House," "A
"Cottage or
books whos
unrelated t
to an even
prominent
and, of cou
him, in sev
such feate
rendered i
In com
Victorian
effect. The
the frame
braces fur
architectu
least as fa
and imita
out most
occasiona
frames, r
impressio
refer to it
Holly
America
(1836-19
a success
when firs
was perh
seven edi
Unfor
neglecte

series of articles entitled "Modern Dwellings: Their Construction, Decoration, and Furniture" that appeared in *Harper's New Monthly Magazine*, beginning in May 1876. As noted earlier, Wheeler had used similar magazine articles as a means of gauging public acceptance before committing his ideas and designs to more permanent form, and much the same course had been followed by Calvert Vaux and others.

To the extent that his purpose in publishing the articles in *Harper's* was to attract comment and criticism, Holly was eminently successful—though perhaps not in just the way he had hoped. The *American Architect and Building News* for July 8, 1876, for example, called him to account for using the work of Eastlake and others without giving credit, labeling his actions "piracy of the most discreditable kind." In reply, Holly freely acknowledged his error, while at the same time claiming that it had been inadvertent and promising that the oversight would be corrected in a forthcoming book. Two years later, with better acknowledgment of his sources and a variety of other changes, he published the articles from *Harper's* under the title *Modern Dwellings in Town and Country*.[32]

The basic fabric of the houses Holly illustrated in *Modern Dwellings* reflected the half-timber style revived in England by Richard Norman Shaw (1831–1912) and John James Stevenson (1831–1908), to which American architects were apt to add a variety of decorative details based on those used by Eastlake for his furnishings and interiors. The resultant style came to be known as "Queen Anne"—not because it resembled closely the style identified with the reign of that monarch, but because the architecture of both periods exhibited a similar mingling of classical and late medieval forms. For his part, Eastlake found much of the American architecture associated with his name "extravagant and bizarre,"[33] while Montgomery Schuyler (1843–1914), the leading American architectural critic of the day, characterized the style as a kind of architectural chaos ("Babel" was his word).[34] Despite such criticism, from the late 1870s through the 1890s, the Queen Anne style enjoyed a widespread popularity, for which Holly was in part responsible as its "literary apostle."[35]

Through his books, Holly's designs must at one time or another have been reflected, directly or indirectly, in scores—perhaps hundreds—of American houses, most of which have since been demolished or altered beyond recognition. This is not to suggest, of course, that Holly's influence on American architecture was solely through his books. Of the 34 designs in *Country Seats*, at least a dozen reflect specific commissions, and there were clearly others. Of these, several were illustrated in the pages of the *American Architect and Building News*, among them the large Queen Anne house in Stamford, Connecticut, that Holly had designed for Henry Robinson Towne, president of the Yale Lock Manufacturing Company. Towne's handsome residence has been demolished, but some impression of its appearance can be gained from the views of the facade and large living hall, complete with fireplace, published in the *American Architect* for November 1879. Three similar, if slightly less pretentious, houses based on Holly's designs and built in Montclair, New Jersey, are also illustrated in the same periodical for August 27, 1881.

Fortunately, the house for which Holly is best known survives. Located in Llewellyn Park, West Orange, New Jersey—itself one of the first and best preserved of the suburbs that grew up around major American cities beginning in the mid-1850s—the house was designed for Henry C. Pedder about 1881. But it was principally to the fame of its second owner that this many-gabled residence in the Queen Anne taste owes its reputation, and very likely its preservation. Thomas A. Edison not only acquired the house in 1887 but also located his laboratory nearby. Still, it must have been the distinction of its design, rather than the prominence of its occupants, that the year before had prompted a French publisher to include the Pedder house in a handsome photographic compendium of the most notable American buildings.[36]

One of the two commissions[37] noted in Holly's brief obituary in the *New York Daily Tribune* was a house in Colorado, reputedly built at a cost of $400,000, an unusually large sum for that time. The Colorado commission is not identified further, but there can be little doubt it was Rosemount, erected between 1891 and 1893 at Pueblo for the entrepreneur John A. Thatcher and perhaps best described as a 37-room Queen Anne mansion struggling against the rising tide of Richardsonian Romanesque. Set apart from its neighbors by its tower and wraparound veranda, the three-and-a-half-story Rosemount is listed on *The National Register of Historic Places*, as is the boyhood home occupied by the prominent conservationist George

Perkins Marsh from 1805 to 1809. The latter house, in Woodstock, Vermont, Holly enlarged and embellished with numerous details in the Queen Anne taste for the railroad magnate and philanthropist Frederick Billings.

For assistance with the architectural portions of the plates of *Modern Dwellings*, Holly acknowledged his indebtedness to Horatio F. Jelliff (1844–1892), who had been an apprentice in his office and was then probably serving as chief draftsman. In the late 1880s Jelliff became a partner in the firm of Holly & Jelliff and in that role doubtless had a part in such commissions as the Thatcher residence in Colorado and Edison's studio in Llewellyn Park.

Holly died September 5, 1892, as a result of injuries received three years previously in a serious fall at a construction site. His son John Arthur Holly continued to practice architecture for a short time, first in 1893 with C. Wellesley Smith in his father's old office at 111 Broadway, and then from 1894 to 1899 alone. The elder Holly was only 58 when he died, perhaps still young enough to have understood and employed to advantage some of the new architectural concepts that promised to alter profoundly the American scene. More than a decade earlier, when the engaging cottages and villas pictured in *Country Seats* had begun to lose their appeal, it was Holly who led the way in accepting the Queen Anne style that by the time of his death was itself giving way to a more faithful adherence to the Georgian forms of America's colonial past.

GEORGE B. TATUM

OLD LYME, CONNECTICUT
March 1, 1993

Notes

1. Los Angeles, 1956. Apparently relying on obituaries or other contemporary sources, the Witheys credit Holly with work at the Virginia Military Institute at Lexington, but more recent studies make no mention of this (e. g., Royster Lyle, Jr., and Pamela Hemenway Simpson, *The Architecture of Historic Lexington*, Charlottesville, 1977). Aside from several short obituaries and notes, the only discussion of Holly's career to appear previously is that found in Michael Tomlan's helpful introduction to the one-volume reprint of Holly's *Country Seats* and *Modern Dwellings*, part of the Library of Victorian Culture (Watkins Glen, 1977; 2nd printing, 1980).

2. H. H. Holly, *Modern Dwellings*, New York, 1878, 152; see also Holly's obituary in the *New York Daily Tribune*, Sept. 7, 1892, 7.

3. Charles Moses Holly, *Record of the Holly Family in America*, Stamford (Conn.), 1861, as cited by Tomlan, note 2.

4. Obituary, *New York Daily Tribune*. The writer of the obituary gives the address of the Holly residence as between 15th and 16th streets on 5th Avenue.

5. After an earlier failed attempt to create an American counterpart to the Royal Institute of British Architects (chartered 1837), in 1857 a group of architects, meeting in New York, succeeded in founding the American

Institute of Architects, which would thenceforth undertake to set standards and to speak for the architectural profession in America. Beginning in 1865, the architectural curriculum at MIT was organized under the direction of William R. Ware (1832-1915), who left MIT in 1881 to establish a second architectural program in the School of Mines at Columbia College in New York.

6. Richard Morris Hunt (1827-1895) studied intermittently at the École between 1846 and 1854. In 1860 Hunt was followed by Henry Hobson Richardson (1838-1886), usually considered the second American of importance to study at the École. Early on, the principles and practices of the École entered American architectural education through Ware, who had not only spent some time in Hunt's students' atelier but, with a view to establishing the program at MIT, had himself traveled extensively in Europe in order to study architectural training there, especially at the École.

7. If Wheeler's career is discussed here in some detail, it is mainly because so little concerning him is otherwise available in published form. Jill Allibone, writing in the *Macmillan Encyclopedia of Architects*, gives 1815 as his probable date of birth and 1870 as the year of his death. Wheeler's last book was published in 1871, however, and the Royal Institute of British Architects reports that he was carried on its rolls until 1872. In note 5 of his introduction (see note 1 above), Tomlan includes a number of details concerning Wheeler's career not readily found elsewhere.

8. In 1796 John Vanderlyn (1775-1852) was sent by his patron to study painting in Paris, where he remained for five years and to which he later returned. During the eighteenth century, painters who had the means to study abroad had regularly turned to London and the London studio of their countryman Benjamin West (1738-1820).

9. One of Downing's principal reasons for taking his first trip abroad in the summer of 1850 was to visit England and to find there someone like Vaux who would return with him to America as his architectural assistant. A year later, Withers answered an advertisement Downing placed in a London newspaper.

10. In the preface to his *Rural Homes* (New York, 1851), Wheeler gives Norwichtown, Connecticut, as his address, while *The Horticulturist* for June 1849 (Vol. III, 560) identifies him as a "European architect of ability, who has established himself at Hartford."

11. Designed for Henry Boody in 1848 and built the following year, this is also known as the Johnson House (Deborah Thompson, *Maine Forms of American Architecture*, Camden [Maine], 1976, 164, Fig. 66).

12. The piece in *The Horticulturist* is dated April 2, 1849, and Wheeler is still listed as writing from Hartford, but the following year, when the design for the English cottage was republished in *The Architecture of Country Houses*, its author is mentioned in the accompanying text as practicing in Philadelphia. This change in address was apparently caused by Wheeler's commission to provide a "very large, convenient, and elegant" Elizabethan house for Henry Fisher, a prominent Philadelphian (*A Philadelphia Perspective: The Diary of Sidney George Fisher*, Nicholas B. Wainwright, ed., Philadelphia, 1967, 229–230). According to the diarist, his brother Henry had engaged A. J. Downing "to lay out the grounds" of his estate, and it may have been Downing who recommended Wheeler as architect. Fisher's Brookwood was demolished about 1930 and no pictures of it have come to light. In 1850 when Wheeler exhibited at the Pennsylvania Academy of the Fine Arts, his Philadelphia address was given as 70 Walnut Street (Anna Wells Rutledge, *Cumulative Record of Exhibition Catalogues* . . . , Philadelphia, 1955, 251). Aside from Henry Fisher's house no other Philadelphia commissions of Wheeler are known, and by 1851 he is listed as practicing in New York City (*Architects in Practice, New York City, 1840–1900*, Dennis Steadman Francis for the Committee for the Preservation of Architectural Records, 1979).

13. The view that Wheeler was an anonymous contributor to *Godey's* is based on a review in which the writer observes that "the best idea of the contents of [*Rural Homes*] we can present to our readers is to refer them to our own views and illustrations of cottages, furniture, etc. . . ." (*Godey's Lady's Book*, Vol. XLIV [1852], 91).

14. Carl W. Condit credits *Homes for the People* with being the first book to take note of the new balloon construction that had been developed in Chicago in the early 1830s and that in time would transform the building industry (*American Building Art: The Nineteenth Century*, New York, 1960, 23).

15. *The Horticulturist*, Vol. VIII (Vol. III of the New Series), 1853, 373–375.

16. Patrick Barry (1816–1890) was an Irish emigrant who became a distinguished pomologist and a partner with George Ellwanger in the highly successful Rochester nursery known as The Mount Hope Botanical and Pomological Garden. Barry edited *The Horticulturist* from the fall of 1852 to the spring of 1855.

17. With a number of different partners, Duggin continued to practice in New York City until 1888 (Dennis Steadman Francis, *Architects in Practice*) and is credited with designing more than 250 city and country houses in the course of his career (Henry and Elsie Withey, *Biographical Dictionary*).

18. Holly was elected Dec. 7, 1857 (*AIA Proceedings, 1857–1871*, as quoted by Tomlan, note 10). He was later made a Fellow of the Institute.

19. According to Jane B. Davies in her new introduction to the Da Capo reprint of *Rural Residences* (New York, 1980). Born in New York City, Alexander Jackson Davis (1803–1892) was arguably the most talented delineator among the American architects of his day. In that role he assisted with the wood engravings that illustrate all of Downing's books.

20. Henry-Russell Hitchcock, *American Architectural Books*, Minneapolis, 1962.

21. In using the word "treatise" in this context Holly may have had in mind the title of Downing's first book, *A Treatise on the Theory and Practice of Landscape Gardening Adapted to North America*, which, in turn, was a conscious echoing of two of the books by the important English landscape gardener Humphry Repton (1752–1818). The term "landscape architect" did not come into use until the 1860s, when it was coined by Calvert Vaux to identify those who produce designs in open space.

22. Waring survived the war and went on to a distinguished career as a civil engineer. Included among his most notable commissions were a number in collaboration with Frederick Law Olmsted (1822–1903), the leading American landscape architect and city planner of the second half of the nineteenth century (*The Papers of Frederick Law Olmsted*, Vol. III, Charles E. Beveridge and David Schuyler, eds., Baltimore, 1983, 105–106). Tomlan (note 13) points out that, like Holly, Waring was a resident of Stamford.

23. *Royal Institute of British Architects Journal*, 1867–1868, 117–128, 167–189. The writer is indebted to Pamela H. Simpson for sharing both this reference and the letter from the RIBA mentioned in note 7, above. Wheeler's London office was located at 9 Conduit Street.

24. Also in Brunswick, Wheeler was engaged in 1855 to decorate portions of the Bowdoin College Library and Chapel, which had recently been completed from designs of Richard Upjohn and which survives as a notable example of the latter's work in the Romanesque style.

25. In America, the Society of Architectural Historians was not founded until 1940, and even then there was considerable doubt as to what to call the discipline it was intended to serve.

26. Tomlan, note 21.

27. Holly did not claim that any railroad station had been built from his designs. Indeed, his principal commissions of a public or institutional nature appear to have been the two buildings he provided for the University of the South at Sewanee, Tennessee—the Hodgson Library and St. Luke's Memorial Hall, of which only the latter survives.

28. The architect favored by the New York Ecclesiological Society (founded 1848) was Frank Wills (1822–1846), an English emigrant who established his New York office in 1849. In 1850 Wills published his *Ancient Ecclesiastical Architecture*, which, together with his numerous articles, significantly influenced the design of American churches, especially those of the Anglican communion.

29. Downing's Bracketed Mode was as near as he came—or ever claimed to come—to developing a distinctly American style.

30. Wheeler's most noteworthy use of the exposed wooden frame was for the house he designed for Henry Olmsted in East Hartford, Connecticut, and later illustrated in *Rural Homes*. The original has not survived but another based on it has. The Willows, built for Joseph Warren Revere in 1850 outside Morristown, New Jersey, is now the property of the Morris County Park Commission (Nancy E. Strathern, "The Willows," *Nineteenth Century*, Vol. 10, 8–11).

31. So named by the Yale historian Vincent Scully, Jr., in *The Shingle Style and the Stick Style*, rev. ed., New Haven, 1971.

32. *Modern Dwellings in Town and Country Adapted to American Wants and Climate with a Treatise on Furniture and Decoration*, New York, 1878. There was at least one reprinting.

33. As quoted by Marcus Whiffen, *American Architecture Since 1780: A Guide to the Styles*, Cambridge (Mass.), 1969, 124.

34. "Recent Building in New York," *Harper's Magazine*, 67 (Sept. 1883), 557–578; reprinted in *American Architecture and Other Writings by Montgomery Schuyler*, William H. Jordy and Ralph Coe, eds., Cambridge (Mass.), 1961, Vol. II, 453.

35. So characterized by Montgomery Schuyler as quoted by Jordy and Coe, *American Architecture*, Vol. I, 73, note 114.

36. *L'Architecture Américaine*, André, Daly fils et Cie, 1886; reprinted as *American Victorian Architecture*, with a new introduction by Arnold Lewis and notes by Keith Morgan, Dover Publications, New York, 1975, Vol. III, 11.

37. The other commission singled out for mention in the obituary was for the Virginia Military Institute, but it was suggested earlier (note 1, above) that this appeared to be an error. Perhaps the writer confused VMI with the University of the South at Sewanee, Tennessee.

PREFACE

————◆◆————

THIS work was fully prepared for the press some two years since, and was about being put into the hands of publishers, when the "War for the Union" broke out, and seemed for a time to paralyze any new enterprise; the author, therefore, thought proper to postpone the publication, until affairs should be in a more settled state, which, although not fully realized at the present time, yet as business has so far become based upon a war footing, the ball is kept rolling, and fortunes appear to be made even faster than in times of peace.

We did intend, as hinted in Design No. 1, giving with this work a Treatise on Landscape Gardening, which, with maps, was commenced under the auspices of Mr. George E. Waring, jr., late of the Central Park; but that gentleman having accepted a commission in the army, the plan was unfortunately abandoned.

The lithographic views, which are signed by Paul Schulze, were in no way designed by him, but simply copied on stone from drawings by the author. One or two of these, in a few of the copies, have a slight mistake in the ground plans, which was not discovered until a small number were printed.

HENRY HUDSON HOLLY,
Architect.

NEW YORK, *Jan. 1st, 1863.*

CONTENTS.

ment.   Description of interior.   How to keep the chambers cool in summer.
Deafening.

DESIGN No. 10.

HOLLY'S

COUNTRY SEATS.

SOME ACCOUNT OF THE HISTORY OF ARCHITECTURE.

ARCHITECTURE, " the first and noblest of the arts," arose with the first wants of mankind. With their earliest ideas of self-dependence, we may reasonably suppose men began to look around them for shelter and protection alike from heat and cold. The refuge of caves and natural excavations could suffice for their uses only while in the most savage state. The first step toward civilization was to create artificial habitations—to build. How rude and insufficient must have been these first attempts we may well judge, when we consider what structures sheltered the descendants of these primeval builders even within the memory of history, and the cabins and huts even now dwelt in by some remote tribes of the wilderness. What plans they adopted, what systems of construction, if any, they pursued, can only be conjectured. The origin of architecture, like all other antediluvian sciences, is involved in obscurity. We know from its nature that it is eminently a progressive science ; and, tracing it backward, step by step, we may arrive at an approximate idea of its earliest feeble efforts. Such a retrospect is not only instructive, but encouraging, reminding us, as it does, of the errors of the rude infancy of architecture, and compelling us to respect the innate strength and manifest destiny of an art which, through innumerable difficulties, could steadily advance from primeval simplicity to its present perfection, where it claims the highest rank among the noblest of human sciences, and points to monuments of its success, not surpassed in excellence by those of any sister art.

The probability is, that nothing more substantial than wood, the skins of beasts, or other equally simple materials, formed the primitive dwellings of mankind.   Scripture informs us that Cain built a city; but that it was constituted of anything more permanent than tents is doubtful.   Not till the building of the Tower of Babel, do we hear of the use of any more noble material.   In this case we are told that burnt brick and slime were used, and it is probable that some previous experience in the working of these materials had been obtained in the erection of less important structures.   We next read of the city of Babylon; but the account is brief and unsatisfactory, throwing no light upon the subject.

The next styles which arose were the Persian, Egyptian, and Indian, the former of which is sometimes called Persepolitan, from Persepolis, in which city are found the principal remains of this style.   It bears some resemblance to the other two in general character, but differs materially in detail.   In each country we find temples of considerable extent, and sepulchral chambers, or catacombs, hewn out of the solid rock, and the walls adorned with hieroglyphics, the records of an advanced state of civilization.   In Egypt these structures contain numerous apartments, while in Persia they are comparatively small, but excel in elaborate porticos richly embellished with sculpture.   Another similarity consists in the massive proportions of these rock-hewn temples and tombs, all seeming to point to a common origin.   The sculpture of Persia and Egypt is also of like character—stiff, formal, and exceedingly laborious; and this fact, in connection with the arrow-headed characters common to both styles, presents a good argument in favor of their relationship.

Egypt, like other primeval nations, has its history shrouded in mystery, and, like that of early Rome, so entangled with the web of mythology, that it is impossible to distinguish truth from fable.   It is, therefore, a matter of uncertainty which of these nations should receive the credit of the earliest attention to architecture; but, judging from the specimens found in the ruins of Babylon, it would seem to be due to that city—these being of a ruder construction than those of Egypt and India, and bearing intrinsic evidence of greater antiquity. For the same reason we would place Egypt second in point of time.

Manetho informs us that the irruption of the *Hyksos*, or shepherd-kings, into Egypt, is supposed to have occurred at about the close of the sixteenth dynasty, and that the seventeenth was under these monarchs. It is at this time that the erection of extensive edifices is presumed to have begun. The usurping shepherds were overpowered by the Pharaohs about 2,000 years b. c., and then commenced the rebuilding of those temples, the magnificent remains of which are the wonder and delight of the traveller even to the present day.

The most noted erections are those whose remains are found in the Egyptian cities along the Nile, and of these, especially Thebes and the Island of Pytæ; yet all contain most interesting specimens of temples, monuments, tombs, sphinxes, and pyramids, delicately sculptured in the hardest granite, and ponderous and herculean beyond any subsequent efforts of the chisel.

The next system, in chronological rotation, appears to be the Grecian, the origin of which is almost as obscure as that of the nation itself. Many authors claim for the Greeks great originality of design; yet there is much reason to suppose them indebted for their first inspirations to the sources we have specified. While denying, however, their originality in architecture, we must admit that in their hands it attained its highest degree of purity, chastity, and grandeur; so that even to the present day their architectural details are imitated, as far more refined and beautiful than any which have since been invented. To this wonderful nation are attributed the three principal orders of architecture, the Doric, Ionic, and Corinthian.

The proportions of the first, we are told, were taken from the figure of a man, its height being six times its diameter—the same ratio that a man's foot bears to his height. This order differs from the other two in the absence of a base. Vitruvius fancifully says that the base was introduced into the Ionic order to represent the sandal, or covering of a woman's foot, and that to the Doric, which represents the strong, muscular, barefooted man, this member is inappropriate.

It is not surprising that a people like the versatile and elegant Greeks should soon weary of a single stereotyped style, repeated with but slight modifications in all their buildings, and long for a change in both order and design. It was to meet this demand that the Ionic order arose. It was invented by the Ionians, as its name implies. The Vitruvian account, sufficiently poetical to be exceedingly improbable, is, " that in erecting the temple of Diana, the proportions and dress of the Goddess were studied. The diameter of the columns was made an eighth part of their height; the base, with folds representing the shoe; the capitals, with volutes, in form of the curled hair worn upon the right and left; and the cymatium, for the locks pending on the forehead from the crown; the flutes in the column are supposed to represent the folds in the drapery." Yet *motives* for all these features are found in the remains of Persepolis and Egypt.

Although there are extant no examples of the Corinthian order at Corinth, yet its name would seem sufficient to entitle that city to the honor of its birthplace. Vitruvius' account of the origin of its capital is a well-known and pretty fable: " Callimachus, an Athenian sculptor, passing the tomb of a young virgin, observed an acanthus growing around the sides of a basket, covered with a tile, and placed upon the tomb; and seeing that the tops of the leaves were bent downward, in the form of volutes, by the resistance of the tile, he took the hint, and executed some columns with foliated capitals, near Corinth, of a more slender proportion than those of the Ionic, imitative of the figure and delicacy of virgins." Unfortunately, however, Egypt is full of the prototypes of this composition.

These three may well be called the basis of all trabeated and columnar architecture; for, whatever changes have been wrought upon them—however much the originals may seem to be lost from view in the multitudinous fancies of subsequent artists, still, divested of all their superfluities, the later productions invariably reduce themselves to one of these.

In this connection it may not be inappropriate to speak of a most remarkable fact in this art. The earliest monuments of the sister arts have passed away; nothing is left, save tradition, by which to judge of the first stages of their existence. The Grecian and Roman empires, where the arts were most cultivated, have declined and fallen, and with them a great part of their history. Little remains even of description, and still less of reality, to guide us in the study of their great achievements. But Architecture nevertheless has survived, an indelible, majestic, and authentic record of their intellectual and moral culture, and the progress of their civilization. It is an art which most closely and intimately unites the beautiful with the useful—a deliberate growth out of the necessities of nations. Were its only object an æsthetic one, its earlier monuments would long ago have disappeared; for it is not in the nature of man habitually to render immortal the "unsubstantial pageants" of the mind. They will not build for beauty, but rather beautify in building. Therefore the adaptation of architecture to the wants of mankind is not only the secret of its beauty, but of its durability also. We may confidently expect that hereafter, as hitherto, this great art will keep pace with the growing grandeur and magnificence of nations, and we may anticipate architectural achievements which, in refinement, splendor, and dignity, will surpass all that our researches in the past can give.

During the administration of Pericles, art made rapid strides. His character, as described by Plutarch, coincides most remarkably with the style of the temples erected by him. He is represented as exhibiting " an elevation of sentiment, a loftiness and purity of style, a gravity of countenance, jealous of laughter, a firm and even tone of delivery, and a decency of dress which no vehemence of speaking ever put in disorder." Athens was at this time nominally a republic, but Pericles was in fact a king; and when the people complained of his lavish expenditures, he replied, " Be mine, then, alone the cost; but, mark ye, be mine alone the glory. Not an Athenian shall be praised, not an Athenian obtain the homage of worship by posterity, when it contemplates these enduring monuments. Not to Athens shall belong the praise of those temples raised to the honor of her deities. No; my name alone shall be inscribed on them, and the city Athens shall live only in the fame of the citizen Pericles." " No!" exclaimed the united voice of the people; " be yours and ours the glory. Draw on the treasury as you will." This anecdote well serves to illustrate the spirit which animated the Grecian architect.

But it is in ancient Rome we must look for the greatest variety and

magnificence in architecture. In the time of Romulus, the dwellings of
the inhabitants were of the rudest description. Ancus Martius was the
first king who commenced work on a larger and more substantial scale.
All succeeding rulers bestowed more or less attention upon this art.
When Greece was overrun by Roman legions, the conquered provinces
retaliated with their architecture, and in a short time overturned all previous systems in Italy, and became in art the masters of the conquerors.
Augustus may be called the Pericles of Rome. He it was who conceived
the idea of making it the most splendid city in the world; and in his day
she attained her highest point of glory in this art. Architects flocked
from Greece to tender their services in beautifying the city, and, by their
aid, Augustus was able to see the realization of his dreams, and to boast
" that he found Rome built in brick, and left it in marble." After Augustus architecture fell into a decline, and did not revive until the reign
of Vespasian. The Coliseum, which was begun by him and finished by
Titus, still stands as one of the wonders of the world. Of all the buildings of ancient Rome, the Pantheon is perhaps most worthy of note. It
was erected by Agrippa, and, as the name indicates, was dedicated to all
the gods. This building will serve as an illustration of some principles of
Roman architecture, as distinguished from Grecian. Its decorations are
of the Corinthian order, and the interior is about 140 feet in height and
diameter. The roof is vaulted; and it is in this system of construction—
that of the arch—that Rome can claim its only title to originality. The
dome is constructed of brick, rubble, and pumice stone, and has a clear
internal diameter of 140 feet, with a circular aperture at the top of 30
feet diameter, which supplies the whole building with light and air, there
being no windows. Around the inside walls are several niches, each
adorned with two columns composed of antique yellow marble, and the
whole interior lining of the walls, as far as the springing of the dome, is
of the finest marble.

Writers, in speaking of the Grecian orders, generally add to them two
others, said to have originated in Rome, viz., the Tuscan and the Com-
posite. The former, of Etruscan origin, is in reality no more than a
clumsy imitation of the Doric, before the Greeks came to teach Rome the
true principles of that style; and the latter is a combination of the Ionic

and Corinthian. The chief, if not the only merits of the old Roman architecture, are its variety and magnificent extent. It possesses little of that strong, meaning, and simple elegance, that refined dignity, so characteristic of the Greek school. Constructive expression and architectural truth were evidently not its aims; and the noble columns supporting massive entablatures in Greece, became here merely ornamental appendages. The arch sustaining all the weight, the columns stand idle and useless on either hand. Of the Romans it has been said, " They emblazoned their imperial city with a thousand splendid errors." Roman architecture typifies Roman pride and ostentation. Here are triumphal arches with bas-reliefs, commemorative of the triumphs of kings and conquerors, and designed to perpetuate their fame, but subserving no loftier purpose; columns, to support only the memory of barbarous conquests; theatres, stadia, and basilicas, to make more magnificent the daily life of a presumptuous and tyrannical people.

It has been said, and not without truth, that the arts are a mirror in which we may see reflected the character of a people; and indeed, as regards architecture, it is an indelible reflection. Every great era in the world's history has left its lasting image on the mirror of this art. If we would know the secrets of the past, we have but to look on the monumental records of Architecture, Sculpture, and Painting. But, among all political changes, none has had a more marked influence on every department of art than the introduction of Christianity. On architecture, especially, has it left its indelible impress; and, through its inspiration, mediæval builders in the midst of Dark Ages built temples of worship so full of beautiful persuasion, that the people entered these gates of promise and joyfully received the baptism of the new faith. Religion, indeed, had always been the principal source—except, perhaps, in Rome—of the highest architectural efforts; and in the idolatrous temples of Greece, Egypt, and India, we may behold the most sumptuous expressions of human intellect in art. But it was reserved for Christian architecture to symbolize a higher aspiration, which only a faith revealed from the Deity himself was capable of conceiving.

Thus originated what is called the Gothic, the first stage of which, from its close relationship with Roman precedents, was known as the

Romanesque, including the Byzantine, Lombardic, Saxon, and Norman, each of which we propose very briefly to describe.

Constantine was the first of the Roman emperors to embrace Christianity; and, that he might with more freedom establish the new religion, he transferred the seat of government to Byzantium. Here, in the effort to throw off all influence of paganism, and to disclaim all connection therewith, a new order of architecture was instituted. Christianity rapidly achieved new triumphs, and spread far and wide, so that in a little more than two hundred years, from Constantine to Justinian, eighteen hundred churches were erected. Christianity soon extended through the entire Eastern Empire, and everywhere this style of architecture, which was the symbol and expression of the new dispensation, accompanied its triumphant progress.

In the reign of Justinian, the Ostrogoths were driven out of Italy, and, the Eastern and Western Empires being thus brought under the rule of one sovereign, the way was opened for the introduction of Byzantine architecture, which, however, did not gain a firm footing in the West till the building of the famous basilica of St. Mark in Venice, in the latter part of the tenth century, though Byzantine builders had been employed in Italy, in works of less importance, many years before this. It is a common error to suppose that Byzantine architecture ever became thoroughly acclimated in Italy. We do not think its efforts were ever very strongly felt outside of Venice, except, perhaps, in some matters of detail. A natural confusion arises from the neglect of the fact, that both Byzantine and Lombardic had a common origin, and therefore in many points were identical. The pure Byzantine seems to have held sway in the East until the invasion of the Ottomans.

Mr. Hope, in speaking of the churches of Byzantium, says: "Arches rising above arches, and cupolas over cupolas, we may say that all which in the temples of Athens was straight, angular, and square, in the churches of Constantine became curved and rounded, concave within and convex without."

The plan of the Byzantine church is what is called a Greek cross; that is, having the arms of equal length. A double dome is placed over the intersection of these arms, the ends of which are covered with conchas, or semi-domes, abutting against the main central cupola. The porticos are invariably omitted, and semicircular arches are everywhere prevalent.

The Lombardic, which, like its rival, the Byzantine, had its origin in the same early Christian Romanesque, derived its name from the circumstance of its prevalence during the supremacy of the Lombards in Italy, and not from its invention being due to them ; since it was developed by the native architects of Italy, and was most in vogue from the seventh to the thirteenth century. The arts flourished in Italy under the Lombardic government, which continued till the time of Charlemagne (A. D. 774), during which period Central Italy became studded with churches and baptistries. This style does not appear to have obtained in Rome. Architecture received a severe check from the incursions of the Saracens from the south, and the discords of rival princes of the north, and did not recover until the eleventh century. From this, until the pointed style was introduced in the thirteenth century, the Lombardic, though somewhat modified, especially prevailed. There are two features which principally distinguished this from the Byzantine, viz., the bell tower, or campanile, and the substitution of the Latin for the Greek cross, as a characteristic form.

The Saxon was the first system of any importance in England, and prevailed from the time of the conversion of the Saxons until the Norman conquest. Doubtless it had its source in the style introduced during the Roman supremacy, as it is hardly to be presumed that either Britons or Saxons had any architecture of their own.

Gregory the Great is believed to have been the first to encourage Christianity in England. We are told he gave permission to St. Augustine to use the pagan temples for purposes of Christian worship.* Within less than fifty years after the death of this great and successful propagandist, the great cathedrals of London, Rochester, and York, and the Abbey of Westminster, were erected, and the more modern structures now occupying the sites of these cathedrals are dedicated to the same saints. The foundations still bear traces of the antique Saxon masonry.

---

* It is well to observe here, that all the earliest Christian temples of worship in Rome were originally the ancient basilicas, or courts of justice, which were admirably suited for the forms of the early ritual of the Church. From these basilicas are directly descended the later cathedral plans with which we are familiar.

The Norman was the Lombardic transplanted into the north of France, and there receiving characteristic modification from the manly energy of the people, and the necessities of the ruder climate. It went over to England with the conquerors, and soon prevailed everywhere throughout the island, absorbing those features of the Saxon style which had in them enough of the elements of life to render them worth preserving. It much resembles the Lombardic, differing from it especially in the absence of the dome or cupola, nor has it the low pedimental roof extending over the whole façade. The sloping arcade in the gable is absent, as likewise the tiers of external galleries or arches. Circular windows are more common, nor do we meet with the peculiar projecting porch, having its columns resting on the backs of animals. Other of its details agree with the Saxon in its massive proportions, the shape of its arches and piers, and its general construction. It is, however, a much more cultivated style than any of the Romanesque schools. It flourished in England from the middle of the eleventh to the end of the twelfth century. After the arrival of William of Normandy, churches were erected in almost every city, village, and hamlet, throughout the island. The latter period of this style has been termed the Semi-Norman, and is important as forming a connecting link between the Romanesque and the Pointed, or Gothic, its principal medium being the pointed arch, which was first introduced about the time of Richard I., when the Crusaders, who are sometimes supposed to have brought this arch from the East, gave a new impulse to Christian architecture. The origin of this pointed arch has for a long time been a subject of controversy; and the minds of archæologists appear now to be pretty generally inclined to the belief that it was not an importation, but a natural constructive development from the old round arch, dimly foreshadowed, a century before it prevailed, so extensively as to be the leading feature of a new system of architecture.

This Gothic or Pointed style, which grew out of and immediately succeeded the Semi-Norman, was expressive in the highest degree of the then prevailing religion. All lines now tended upward, and each member appeared expressive of some mark of the Christian faith. The plan of the church was a cross, which also appeared conspicuous in its various details. Trefoil arches and panels, typifying the Trinity, soon became prominent. The substantial buttress, which gave strength to the walls, now ran above the roof, and finished with a pinnacle. Instead of heathen domes, the Christian spire towered upward, pointing to the heaven of which Faith whispers. Mr. Wightwick, in alluding to this beautiful thought, says : " All that you saw ere you entered the gate of Constantinal Rome, only sought to inform you of the grandeur and the grace belonging to those idolatrous creations, which, however lofty, still maintain but a horizontal course with Earth : nor was it till the genius of Pointed Design expanded itself in the glowing atmosphere of Christianized Europe, that Architecture aspired to raise the eye above the level of mere human perfection, and to give it a 'heaven-directed' aim. Then sought she, in the long vistas and mounting spires which distinguish the wondrous temples of Germany, France, and Great Britain, to symbolize the ever-vanishing perspective of Eternity, and the infinite altitude of the Creator above his creatures. Their lofty pillars seemed rather to spring *from* the earth, than to rest *upon* it ; their aspiring arches, instead of downward pressure, expressed upward continuity ; and those windowless walls, which in the Heathen temple remained in stubborn solidity to exclude the light, were now pierced on all sides to admit the beams of divine day. Now sought they to typify, by the sobered splendor of emblazoned glass, how, through the many-colored medium of mystery, heaven poured its dazzling rays, in mercy dimmed for mortal eyes. Now, sought they, in their cruciform plan, to exhibit a symbol of the Everlasting sacrifice, and in their central crowning tower, an abiding monument of Salvation ; whilst, like ever-soaring piety, upward and still upward rose the 'star-y-pointing' spire, to seek its *finial* in that heaven where alone the soul's consummation *can* be sought."

The words of Coleridge, in comparing the Classic and Gothic modes of architecture, are remarkable : " The Greek art is beautiful. When I enter a Greek church, my eye is charmed, and my mind elated ; I feel exalted, and proud that I am a man. But the Gothic art is sublime. On entering a cathedral, I am filled with devotion and with awe ; I am lost to the actualities that surround me, and my whole being expands into the infinite ; earth and air, nature and art, all sweep up into eternity, and the only sensible impression left is, that I am nothing."

If, in describing the various eras of Gothic architecture, we seem to lay too little stress on its continental developments in France, Germany, and Italy, we are not to be understood as undervaluing the latter. On the contrary, we are ready to state that these continental developments were always in advance of the English a quarter of a century or more, and in quality and quantity perhaps, in magnificence and costliness, far surpassed those of our mother country. But the limit to which we have restricted ourselves in this brief historical sketch, scarcely permits our following the progress of architecture everywhere, and so we have thought proper to confine our attention to the English, as being nearer our own sympathies, less likely to confuse our readers with a multitude of examples, and, at the same time, containing all the essential characteristics, signally expressed, which constitute mediæval or Gothic architecture.

It is the custom to divide English Gothic as follows : *Early English*, from A. D. 1189 to 1307, or during the reigns of Henry II., Richard I., John, Henry III., and Edward I. *Decorated English*, from A. D. 1307 to 1377, or during the reigns of Edward II., Edward III., and Richard II. *Perpendicular English*, from A. D. 1377 to 1460, or during the reigns of Henry IV., V., and VI.

The first of these, which we shall call the style of the thirteenth century, is distinguished by long and narrow lancet-headed windows, employed singly or collectively ; being in the latter case separated by narrow piers. The heads are decorated with concentric tables or dripstones. The buttresses have much greater projection than in the Norman examples, where they were rarely larger than the pilasters of the classic temples. Large columns of this style are seldom seen, save in the form of a series of small ones clustered. Examples of this period are exceedingly beautiful, simple, and elegant in design, and delicate in execution, equally applicable to the modest village church and the noble abbey or cathedral ; remarkable in the one case for unpretending simplicity, and in the other for solemn and majestic grandeur.

The second of these divisions, which is called the Decorated, or middle pointed Gothic, may be classed as the style of the fourteenth century. This period excels all the others in point of beauty. It not only rivals the preceding in chastity, but surpasses it in richness, without being overburdened with the extravagant and unmeaning ornamentation of the styles which followed. In this the narrow, lancet-headed windows, grouped together, as in the former style, and separated by narrow piers, are clustered into one imposing window, with one arch surmounting the whole and filled up with tracery, composed in the most graceful combinations, in which are introduced cuspidations or foliations in nearly every possible variety. The increased richness of these windows warranted a corresponding decoration of the entire building. Enriched crockets, or bunches of carved leaves, were soon employed, running up the sloping angles of gables and spires, and terminating in an ornamental finial which surmounted the whole.* These ornaments, though chaste, were still superfluous, and soon degenerated into extravagant, unmeaning decoration, the invariable precursor of declining art. This was soon evident in the Perpendicular, whose origin dates at the close of the fourteenth century, and which prevailed till the almost total disuse of Gothic architecture in England. It was characterized by its excess of ornaments, forming a marked contrast with the former styles. The term Perpendicular was given it on account of the peculiar arrangement of the tracery in the window heads, and in the panels with which every surface was filled, this tracery being composed exclusively of upright bars connected by foliated heads. This name has, however, been objected to as of only partial application, and the term Horizontal suggested as more appropriate and significant of the general tendency of the style; and this idea seems well founded, for here, instead of the uplifted arch and the uniform upward tendency, alluded to as features of the preceding styles, we have the depressed arch, low roof, square-headed windows and doorways, square hood mouldings and horizontal transoms, all imparting a flat and level appearance. Even spires were abandoned, elaborately finished towers being substituted, which were sometimes surmounted by lanterns.

King's College Chapel, Cambridge, and Henry the Seventh's Chapel at Westminster, are the most elaborate examples in England of the Perpendicular system. It is worthy of note that this style is so prevalent among the collegiate buildings of England, especially at Oxford and Cambridge, as, through association, to have become almost classic. Few eras

* For an early English design of the thirteenth century, see No. 32; while Design No. 33 is of the Decorative, or fourteenth century.

of building are so open to criticism as this; but its practical results are such that, perhaps, no other one is so endeared to the hearts of the English people. This may be owing partly to the fact that the Perpendicular, unlike the other styles, was not derived from the Continent, but is exclusively English in all its characteristics; the contemporary style in France being the Flamboyant, where the tracery seems to wave and flare like the wildest flames; and in Germany, the Geometrical, the tracery being composed merely of geometrical lines, infinitely combined from angular and circular elements, and foliated. The cathedrals of Beauvais, St. Ouen, and part of Rouen, may be considered the representative buildings of the Flamboyant; while those of Cologne and Strasburg occupy the same position in the geometrical style of Germany.

Domestic architecture in England may be said to have arisen in the time of Henry VII. With his reign was inaugurated an entire change in the life and habits of the English people. With his marriage the feuds of York and Lancaster ceased, and a long season of peace seemed about to follow the internal discords which had distracted the reigns of his predecessors. Previous to this period, domestic architecture had scarcely an existence, save in the form of fortified castles. Henry VIII. did much to revolutionize the art, for during his reign the Reformation was established in England, and the sacrilegious plunder and destruction of monasteries and religious houses, carried on under his orders, discouraged the erection of new, while it removed the old examples. But, while he was thus a destroyer of the works of antiquity, he was a liberal patron of the new architecture, and erected many palaces and civic buildings.

It is not surprising that, when a monarch initiated a movement of this kind, his subjects should continue it. Foremost in such works, therefore, was the great Cardinal Wolsey, by whose power and lavish expenditure were built some of the noblest residences and collegiate buildings in England.

Many novel features were introduced into domestic architecture to meet the new exigencies of the improved social life of those days: among the most prominent of these are bay and oriel windows, chimney stacks, roof ceilings, and panelled wainscots around interior walls.

The Italian style did not prevail extensively in England until some time after it had been established in France under Pierre Lescot, Philibert, Delorme, Jean Bullaut, and other architects of celebrity. In the reign of Henry VIII., and more especially in that of Elizabeth, owing to the increased intercourse with the Continent, Italian details began to work their way into English architecture. It was evident which way the finger of art was pointing. As the mixed architecture of Constantine formed a connecting link between heathen "classic" and Christian "Gothic," so the Elizabethan stood between Christian "Gothic" and the revival of the old classic forms. It has been remarked that, in the mausoleum of Westminster, the pointed style expired in a blaze of glory. It was like the setting of the sun, whose lingering rays play around and illuminate the mountain tops, when their great source has sunk below the horizon.

Holbein initiated the fashion for reviving the styles of Italy in England ; and when Elizabeth ascended the throne she found her architectural realms distracted by a most fierce civil war. The buildings erected in her time are but so many lasting records of desperate actions between the antagonistic principles of the Gothic St. Peter's at York and the classic St. Peter's at Rome.

Perhaps the first indication of a tendency to revive the classic orders was exhibited by *Arnolfo di Cambio da Colle*, in his design for the Cathedral of Florence, which, however, is essentially an Italian Gothic composition in sentiment. But little progress was made in this direction till the time of Brunelleschi, who built the famous dome over that cathedral, and who may be said to be the father of the Italian style. From this period, the beginning of the 15th century, this style extended rapidly throughout Italy.

Italian Renaissance may be divided into three classes, named, from the cities in which they prevailed, Florentine, Roman, and Venetian. That of Florence is peculiar, especially that of her palaces. Strong, massive, and severe, they are rather fortresses than the residences of peaceful merchants. Nor was this appearance needless and deceitful ; for the strength of these mansions was requisite for defence in the midst of the civil strifes and commotions which disturbed the peace of the State until the time of the Medicis. Florentine buildings excel in dignity those of Rome and Venice, but fall far short of them in lightness and elegance ; they are inferior in refinement of detail, but surpass all others in imposing boldness.

"The buildings of Florence," says a French author, "appear to be not the work of ordinary men. We enter them with respect, expecting to find them inhabited by beings of a nature superior to ourselves. Whether the eye is arrested by monuments of the age of Cosmo de Medici, or of the times which preceded or followed it, all in this imposing city carries the imprint of grandeur and majesty. Frequent revolutions oblige the chief parties to consider their personal safety, along with the magnificence of their dwellings. Externally, they are examples of skilful union of grace with simplicity and massiveness. After Rome, Florence is the most interesting city to every artist."

The edifices of modern Rome are of a very different character from those of Florence; they do not possess the massive appearance of the latter, but are distinguished for an air of lightness and elegance. This style forms a connecting link between the Florentine and Venetian; for, while on the one hand it is less heavy and severe than the former, it is, on the other, not so gay and slight as the latter. Bramante, perhaps, was the founder of this style, and the principal examples are the great basilica of St. Peter's and the Farnese palace; the former of which may justly be considered the great achievement of Renaissance. The original design was furnished by Bramante, but was altered by almost every architect employed upon the building. Bramante commenced the erection, but did not proceed far with the work; the body of the church being the work of Peruzzi and San Gallo; the dome, of Michael Angelo and Fontana; the nave and west façade, of Carlo Maderno; the colonnades, of Bernini. The plan was originally a Latin cross, which was changed by Michael Angelo into a Greek cross, and again to the Latin form by Carlo Maderno, called by an indignant and caustic critic, "the wretched plasterer from Como." A few of the dimensions of this building may not be uninteresting, and, in giving them, we shall compare them with those of St. Paul's, of London.

	ST. PETER'S.	ST. PAUL'S.
Whole length of church and porch, ...	729 feet.	500 feet.
Breadth of front with turrets, ...	364 "	180 "
Diameter of cupola, ...	189 "	145 "
Height from ground to top of cross, ...	437½ "	370 "
Top of highest statue on front, ...	175 "	135 "

As before stated, the Venetian Renaissance is characterized by its preëminent lightness and elegance. San Michele or Sansovino may be said to have been the founder of this school, and they were followed by Palladio, Scamozzi, &c. Good examples of these are the Library of St. Mark, the Pamphili palace, Verona, and the Chapel of St. Bernardino.

But Palladio is our model among Italian artists. His style, termed the Palladian, was soon adopted throughout a great part of the Continent, and introduced, in the reign of James I., into England by the celebrated Inigo Jones. In the early part of his practice, this architect had followed the mixed style before described as the Elizabethan, but on his return from a journey to Italy in 1619, he brought back with him the manner of the Palladian school, in which his principal works were executed, as the portico of old St. Paul's, Whitehall palace, York stairs, and the church of St. Paul, Covent Garden. Few of the works of his genius now remain; most of them having been destroyed by the great fire of 1666, or removed to make way for succeeding improvements. This great fire gave an opening for the newly adopted style of architecture, which perhaps would never otherwise have been obtained. Nor was it a small advantage that it received the favor of Sir Christopher Wren, who was undoubtedly a man of superior attainments in his profession.

Space will not allow us to enumerate the sixty churches, the palaces, and other public and private buildings erected by him; but we cannot pass over his *chef d'œuvre*, the Cathedral of St. Paul, without some brief description. This magnificent edifice not only furnishes us with a remarkable specimen of constructive skill, but with a grand example of Italian architecture, as applied to sacred purposes.

Tradition informs us that the site of this building was, at the time of the Roman rule in England, occupied by a temple dedicated to Diana. However this may be, it is certain that one of the earliest Christian churches in England was erected on this spot by King Ethelbert, who had been converted by St. Augustine. This church was destroyed by fire in 961, but was immediately rebuilt. In 1087 it was again consumed in a conflagration, which laid waste the greater part of the metropolis. At this time Maurice, Bishop of London, conceived the grand design of erecting the magnificent edifice which preceded the present cathedral. This was again much injured by fire in 1135, which consumed all of the building that was combustible. The enterprise of the age was not, however, to be repressed, even by such repeated disasters; for, in 1221, the central tower was finished, and in 1229 Bishop Niger undertook to rebuild the choir in a new style of architecture and with enlarged dimensions; this was completed in 1240. This edifice, previous to James I., had been twice struck by lightning and had undergone many changes and repairs; but in his reign it was found to be in a dilapidated condition, and, though large sums of money were collected and material provided for its repair, nothing was done till the reign of Charles I., when Inigo Jones was appointed to superintend the work, which was begun in 1633, and in the course of nine years a magnificent portico was erected on the west front, and the building newly cased in stone. During the time of Cromwell, however, the building was nearly ruined by being converted into stables and barracks. The regular government of the church being restored with the succeeding monarch, the Dean and Chapter proceeded immediately, under the direction of Sir John Durham, to remove all traces of the encroachments begun in 1663. Three years later, this unfortunate building again fell a prey to the flames, which consumed the roof, and so weakened the walls that they were deemed incapable of repair. It was determined to erect a new building, which was commenced in 1675, and in 1710 the last stone was laid by Mr. Christopher Wren, son of the architect. Thus, through a series of most unexampled misfortunes, this church was completed in thirty-five years, under the direction of one architect, and, by a remarkable coincidence, of one master mason, Mr. Strong, and under the auspices of one bishop of London, Dr. Henry Compton.

Of all Wren's pupils, only one attained great eminence, Nicholas Hawksmore, one of whose churches, that of St. Mary, Woolworth, is of considerable merit. The next architect of note, practising this style, was James Gibbs, the architect of St. Martin's-in-the-Fields and St. Mary's-le-Strand, both of which present many good features. Passing by many architects of less note, we may mention Sir William Chambers, who greatly excelled his contemporaries, and many of his predecessors of this school. His greatest work is Somerset House, a description of which we regret being compelled to omit.

Meanwhile, the French Renaissance was brilliantly developing itself in innumerable palaces and churches and civil buildings. In the palaces, especially, are displayed the most original invention and profoundest knowledge of the art of design ever lavished upon the Renaissance. It would be impossible to enumerate and detail all the examples of this era in France, but we would especially signalize the royal chateaux and palaces of Blois, Chambord, Chinonceaux, Fontainebleau, the Tuileries, and the extensions of the Louvre.

The London club houses exhibit some of the most happy attempts at Italian architecture, and are far preferable to ecclesiastical edifices built in this style; a fact arising not so much from the respective merits of the architects employed, as from the better adaptation of the style for that particular class of buildings. It has also of late been adopted for private mansions, both in town and country, for which it seems particularly fitted; but for ecclesiastical structures, colleges, &c., the Gothic designs are rapidly superseding the Italian, while for public buildings for government, and other secular purposes, the Grecian is generally regarded as preferable, though in the great Parliament Houses of London the Perpendicular style has been imitated by Sir Charles Barry.

Architecture, in our own country, has never taken any stand, or received especial attention till within the past few years. But in this brief time it has made unprecedented progress, and bids fair to advance at a much more rapid rate, so that before another century rolls by we shall undoubtedly be able to show an architecture which will be capable of taking its stand by the side of the great historical architectures of the world. To attain this end, we must not be mere copyists of those who have gone before. While we cull from the structures of all ages and countries those features which are applicable to our requirements, we must reject those which to us are without meaning or use, and, at the same time, add whatever may be suggested by the necessities of climate, habits, and education.

To us, then, architecture becomes the most important of the arts, as by it we are destined to express in monumental language our worthiness to occupy a place among the civilized nations of Christendom, and by every consideration, therefore, we urge that it receive, in our colleges and schools, that attention and cultivation to which it is eminently entitled. A knowledge of this art is abroad deemed no less essential than, among us, is that of music or any accomplishment. In England, the youth who could not tell what style of architecture prevailed in any given country would be regarded as we would regard the American lad who is ignorant of an important era or event in our history.

Thus have we, briefly as might be, attempted some description of the rise and progress of this important art. Its details are far too extensive to be more than glanced at in our space, and our only object has been to maintain and illustrate the idea that architecture is an art which, as its foundations are laid in utility, is eminently progressive. A retrospect of its history cannot fail to impress the thoughtful student with the idea that its triumphs under so many and great difficulties demonstrate most satisfactorily its manifest destiny to continue its majestic growth and expansion, as we grow and expand in all the arts of peace and prosperity. Conscious of our own inability worthily to display the beauties of our subject, we shall be amply repaid if by our effort any degree of attention may be attracted to this subject and, in the mind of our reader, our original position sustained, however imperfectly—that " architecture is the first and noblest of the arts."

ADVANTAGES OF A COUNTRY LIFE.

In this country, like those of Europe, more especially that portion inhabited by the Anglo-Saxon race, the inclinations of the people, save where perverted by unwholesome education, seem decidedly in favor of a rural life; already there are many families of culture and refinement who spend all their days in their country homes, or, if they leave them, they do so only for a few months in winter, when nature, disrobed of her more pleasing ornaments, with scourges of snow, and sleet, and bitter cold, drives even her most constant votaries to seek the social comforts of the city. But it is a source of rejoicing when they are reached by the march of spring from the dissipation and the artificialities of town life to the simpler and purer pleasures which she gives. There is another class, which, though compelled to spend the business hours of the day in the city, gladly hasten when these are over to peaceful homes, removed from the bustle and turmoil of the crowded town. This manner of living is becoming very popular, especially among the business community; and now that we have so many and ready means of communication between cities and their suburbs for many miles around, and at so trifling an expense, it is rather to be wondered at that more do not adopt it. The objection that too much time is thus lost in travelling to and fro·is not well founded, since it actually requires but little more to reach a country place twenty miles from town than to go from an office in Wall Street to a residence in the upper part of the city.

It seems scarcely necessary at this day to bring forward any formal arguments in favor of country life. It has beeen the favorite theme of philosophers and poets in all times. Its pure and elevating influences, its comfortable ease, its simplicity and cheapness, have been urged again and again in grave essays and pleasant pastoral and bucolic meditations. Yet there is one consideration to which we, by permission, wish briefly to draw the attention of our readers. We refer to that of health. It is often declared that the human race, at least in this country, is degenerating; and there appears to be some foundation for this remark as applied to our large towns. We look at a tall, muscular, well-developed form, in all its rare physique, rather as the heritage of some heroic past than an expression of life such as we now lead, which seems rather to produce a weak-eyed, narrow-chested race, with sallow complexions, weak constitutions, and, in short, but little physical force. We rather run to brains, and are content to *read* the exploits of Achilles and Hector in our classics, rather than emulate their strength and prowess. We touch with delicate hands the great, rude armor in the Tower, and wonder at the huge-limbed generation which wore it as we do our silk and broadcloth. We are thus forced to inquire why so marked a deterioration has taken place. It has been said that we Americans are not acclimated in this New World; that this decline has been constantly going on from the days of our forefathers. But we need not go back far in time or deep in science to account for this change. The secret lies in our artificial lives. We do not breathe enough of the pure, fresh air of heaven; the little exercise we take is spasmodic and business-like; and, worse than all, we are irregular in our habits, imprudent in diet and exposure, and indulge too freely in the well-known dissipations of city life. In many cases, perhaps in the majority, the leaving of town in the summer is but another phase of the same life, with simply a change of scene from the city to some fashionable watering place, with a repetition of the routine of dress, suppers, and late hours. Such life is unnatural and injurious, simply because it is artificial. If, then, we would leave the city, not for fashion, but for prudence; if we would really recuperate our strength and energies, we must seek the repose of a genuine country home, and those remedies which nature provides with a lavish but never-failing hand.

Let us presume that, influenced by these and the many other considerations which will suggest themselves to the intelligent reader, it is decided to build a home somewhere in the country. Where shall it be? A homestead—for we would not build for ourselves alone, but for those who may succeed us—naturally suggests a place somewhat isolated and independent, rather than a residence on the street of a country town or village: it should be complete in itself, liberal in extent, and free from all intrusions—in fine, a little principality. Do not suppose that such a country home can be secured only by the wealthy, and that those of more moderate means can expect nothing better than a house, elbowed by neighbors, in the closer suburbs of a town, or at most a lot in a village, where one must be content with half an acre of land, and submit ease and domestic quiet to the scrutiny of tattling gossips and the curiosity of the vulgar. The inconveniences and petty annoyances of such life are so well known, that one of limited means, who would make himself a home in the country, would do well to inquire if it is necessary to submit to them, or if they cannot economically be avoided.

It is generally thought that the establishment of a country place, with several acres of land, involves a great original outlay and a large increase of taxes, which, added to the interest on the investment, makes a heavy rent; that a residence of this kind involves the necessity of keeping a horse and conveyance of some kind, and a man servant to take care of them. Now we reply by reminding our readers, that six acres in the country can generally be had for a smaller sum than half an acre in a village, with a proportional difference in taxes. Again, we may safely consider that the produce of a little farm, if prudently managed, will not only support both man and horse, but, with attention, can be made a source of profit, and supply to its owner many luxuries of a superior kind and at little cost. Moreover, in improving the place and elaborating its culture, he obtains a nobler profit than this—an inheritance of happiness and content for his children.

Our country abounds in most interesting and picturesque scenery, embracing ocean, river, lake, and mountain, easy of access, habitable and healthy; and, though filled with delightful villa sites, is too frequently suffered to remain neglected and unpeopled in its choicest nooks. Those proposing to build in the country, are much more likely to select some spot destitute of almost every natural embellishment. There appears to be little appreciative aptitude for the association of homes with natural beauty. If the ground is entirely level, free from rocks, hills, dales, water, and trees, it is claimed and occupied quite as readily as some site equally accessible and adorned with all the picturesque or gentle loveliness of nature—perhaps even more so. People like to *visit* such places, but they *will not live* there. A fine view and romantic scenery seem to be secondary considerations to other and less elevated advantages, such as neighbors, proximity to railway stations, &c. It must be granted, however, that rural taste has greatly improved since the days of Downing. Until the present time the professions of architecture and landscape gardening have been nearly new among us, and practised mostly by strangers; but now that so many young Americans of intelligence and culture are studying and assuming these professions, we may reasonably hope to see more interest taken in them, and the happy revolution, so long delayed, at length realized and effected.

Giving these reflections their due weight, let us now proceed to select a site. Accessibility, neighborhood, and health, are, of course, primary considerations, and in most instances it would be improper to sacrifice any of these, even to the desire to live in the midst of natural beauty. Fortunately, however, we are rarely obliged to go far before we find plenty of locations which combine natural beauty with all the practical advantages we can wish for. We are naturally attracted by fertility of soil; but if we do not propose to establish a productive farm, simply for the sake of its productiveness, it would be well to inquire, before settling in any such locality, about the healthfulness of it; for the most fertile spots are frequently the most insalubrious. Burton, in his "Anatomy of Melancholy," quaintly draws our attention to this fact. "The best soil commonly yields the worst air; a dry, sandy plat is fittest to build upon, and such as is rather hilly, than a plain full of downs; a cotswold country, as being most commodious for hawking, hunting, wood, waters, and all manner of pleasures." After enumerating many such tracts of land, he goes on to say that Stephanus, a Frenchman, agrees with "Cato, Varro, Columella, those ancient rusticks," in the idea that the front of a house should "stand to the south," and approves especially of "the descent of a hill south or southeast, with trees to the north, so that it will be well watered; a

condition in all sites which must not be omitted, as Herbastein incul-
cates."

It is an erroneous idea to suppose that your house must necessarily be
approached by the highway. If you own to the main road, you may, of
course, have your gate entrance on your own land; if not, you have only
to obtain a right of way from your neighbor, and continue your carriage
road through his grounds. There is rarely any difficulty in the way of
obtaining this privilege. In selecting a site, it is well to have higher
ground on the northern and western sides to screen your house in winter
from chilling winds. Do not allow picturesque rocks, or wild forest trees to
influence your decision against any site, as, in case such features appear too
rude for your notions of the elegant repose and gentleness which should
surround your domicil, your landscape gardener can always reconcile them,
domesticate them, as it were; in short, make them beautiful and appropriate; and your architect, if a man of taste and education, can arrange your
house to combine gracefulness with any peculiarities of country, and give
it such character as will be congruous with surrounding scenery.

It is well to warn our readers against adopting any plan of a model
house, or the design in some book, which there may present a pleasing exterior, without careful consideration of its adaptability to their grounds.
Such designs may, perhaps, be suitable in every respect for their intended
site; but when placed on a different one, may be quite the reverse. In
the one case, the kitchen, hall, and minor offices may occupy the least desirable exposures, and obstruct no views, but by their position shelter the
house from wind and storm; in the other, all may be changed. None of the
advantages of the new situation will be improved. The drawing room,
perhaps, looks out upon the farm yard; the dining room, with a fine bay
window, from which originally might have been enjoyed three distinct
views, commands an uninterrupted prospect of the stable, the kitchen garden, or some low, flat, and uninteresting country; while really the only
pleasantly situated room is, fortunately for the servants, appropriated to
their avocations. So, too, the external appearance of the house may be
little fitted for its new position. It may be Italian in style, adapted to a
level, grassy lawn, pleasantly shaded by majestic elms and maples. Your
site, however, is perhaps picturesque, covered wildly with oak, and cedar,

and larches, full of sudden surprises of form and color.   To place an Italian villa here, is like adorning a wigwam with the Venus de Milo.   Let us rather, for such a locality, adopt *motives* from the irregular Gothic, with its pointed roofs, lofty towers and chimneys, and varied outline; or from some other congenial styles.

Though architecture is comparatively so new, and has received so little earnest and serious attention from us as a nation, that we can scarcely be said to have any styles or systems peculiarly our own, yet there have grown out of our necessities certain idiosyncracies of building and design, which are doubtless in the way of establishing that long-dreamed-of aim, an *American style*.   In the absence of such a style, we have been too apt to borrow bodily and without change from those of foreign countries, which are the expressions of the especial needs and social conditions of those countries and those alone.   It is certainly our duty to introduce from abroad methods and manners of design, so far as they meet our wants.   But it would be worse than folly, in building an English cottage, for example, not to have a veranda, because its prototypes in England have none ; we have an actual need for such an appliance in our dry and sunny climate, and it is out of such need that must proceed a distinctive feature of American cottage architecture.   While, therefore, we avail ourselves of all the good points of the different styles, and make ourselves familiar with them, we should not so venerate as to fear to change them when we find that our necessities require it.

Thus, doubtless, we are building up styles of our own, taught, as other founders of styles have been, by precedents in older countries or times.   Our climates, habits, and materials differ enough from those of Europe to demand different architectural arrangements and treatments. For instance, most of our country abounds in timber, a most excellent building material.   In this respect we differ from Europe, where wood is much more rare and expensive.   Yet, in our careless and blind way, we have proceeded to copy in this material, as exactly as we can, the details of foreign architecture, which were intended to express the constructive capacities of stone or brick.   The temples of Greece, built of marble, with their ponderous shafts, entablatures, and pediments, have all been repeated in this country in wood, painted white, and blocked in courses to imitate stone, and often sanded to perfect the intended deception. So, too, with the feudal castles of England; they are here revived, and, with their frowning battlements and towers, are built of the same improper material. The grand old massive cathedrals and churches of by-gone days have not escaped the same indignity. How absurd it must seem to a stranger to see a Roman arch, key-stone and all, imitated in wood, or a buttress of hollow woodwork, or a simple cottage painted to resemble stone. Fortunately, our people are awakening to the folly of this unmeaning imitation, and where stone is adopted it is treated as stone, and where wood is employed we are properly beginning to show details adapted to the material, such as projecting roofs and framed brackets descending from the rafters, with a lighter and more fitting construction of verandas and balconies.

But there are some portions of our country, as in most of the Eastern and Middle States, where wood is by no means abundant. In many localities we have barely enough left for shade, and some of the finest sites have been stripped of their luxuriant and noble growth of trees. We have been wastefully extravagant of our timber, and should now sometimes be at a loss for building materials, had not nature provided another near at hand, and in such profusion that we are really compelled to use it or to remove it from our way. This, we need hardly say, is stone, which is constantly growing in favor and use.

People who build in the country are often like those who plant trees, whose full luxuriance they themselves can never expect to enjoy; and the children who come after them reap the benefit of the generous forethought. When we have procured a rude piece of ground, cleared it, planted it, beautified it, constructed the roads, and erected house, stable, and all the fixtures of a homestead thereon, we cannot realize from its sale the value of our time, trouble, and outlay. The reward is in the comfort of our declining years, and the happiness of our descendants. A country house is a *cheap luxury*, which we buy, build, or inherit for ourselves and our children. Such being the intention, evidently it should be built of the most durable materials. Nor is stone so expensive when we regard its use in a proper light; nay, we may even say it is cheaper in the end. Take, for example, Design No. 9, which cost about $5,000. The owner says his house is perfectly dry, stands in the best manner, and requires much less fuel to warm it than he has been in the habit of using in frame houses of the same size.   With this may be compared a house very similar and of about the same cost, but built of wood, whose owner declares that he is obliged to paint the outside every two or three years to preserve the woodwork and make it appear respectable.   Frequent repairs are also necessary on the exterior ; some of the timbers have sprung, the floors are uneven, and the walls and ceilings cracked.   His roof, which is of shingles, he says frequently leaks, and a new one will soon be required.   These repairs demand no small outlay each year, all of which, with the great attendent inconveniences, might have been avoided, had he built of stone with a slate roof.   A prejudice has extensively prevailed against stone houses on account of their dampness ; an objection which has not been unfounded, but which is now wholly removed by building the outside walls hollow ; that is, using brick furring within a few inches of the external wall, and fastened to it by iron anchors.   The old plan was to nail wooden strips to the inside of stone walls, and lath and plaster upon these ; but this affords no protection from the dampness.   Again, should the outside wall settle, the plaster must be cracked, while the brick furring would settle with the stone ; so, too, the wood furring is apt to shrink from having the warm room on one side and the cold or damp wall on the other.

In Design No. 9, already alluded to, the brick furring is used, thus making it a house within a house ; it has an outside stone wall 18 inches thick, a hollow space of 3 inches, and a brick wall of 4 inches.   The plastering is done on the inside surface of the brick, consequently no lathing is required, and but two coats of plaster instead of three.   This avoids the difficulties spoken of, and is proof from vermin and fire.   The hollow space acts as a perfect ventilating flue throughout the house, and by having outside registers, which can be closed in cold weather, and a register at the floor and ceiling of each room, a constant circulation may be obtained.   It is well to continue this hollow space up to the roof rafters, and the air, following the space between these rafters up to the scuttle between roof and ceiling, will keep the attic perfectly cool in summer.

As to the durability of stone, no argument is, of course, required.   We have only to visit older countries to find walls which have stood hundreds of years, and there is no reason why we may not have them of equal durability. There is an air of dignity and stability about a stone structure, and age, so far from being destructive to it, serves only to increase its solidity and improve its appearance. What can be more beautiful and picturesque than an old stone edifice, overgrown with moss and shaded by noble trees, all indicating that time has but improved the work of art? What would be the case with a wooden structure under similar circumstances? " Decay's effacing fingers " are constantly at work, and walls of wood offer an effectual field for their labors. Frequent and expensive repairs present but feeble resistance to the progress of dilapidation. The building must crumble and fall in the process of a few generations. The wood rots, the roof leaks, the walls and ceilings are cracked by the shrinking and settling of the timbers. With such facts known to us, there can be no doubt which of these two materials is the most suitable and economical. Moreover, vines, the pleasantest adornments of a cottage wall, ivy and woodbine, with which nature seems to take possession of the works of our hands and tenderly take them to her bosom, cling without detriment to stone, while, attached to wood, they are the readiest agents of decay.

But, whatever material you use, remember the maxim, " Truthfulness in building." Let the treatment correspond with the substance with which you build. Do not carve stone details out of wood, nor, with false pride, attempt to make it resemble something else. Above all, do not try to hide the face of stonework with plaster, painted to appear as if dressed. One need never blush at any expression of truthfulness in his dwelling, however homely that expression may be ; but falsehood and imitation give indisputable evidence of vulgarity of taste—*snobbishness* is the modern word.

Having selected the site and chosen the material, the next step is to procure a design best suited to the wants and conveniences of your family, improving the advantages of the finest exposures and views, protecting yourself from the inclement points in winter, and excluding from sight the objectionable portions of the grounds. And we cannot reiterate too often the injunction, that in external treatment the house should harmonize with the surrounding scenery. Can you furnish this design yourself? Decidedly not, unless you have spent years in study and practice. Or, possessing good ideas yourself, can a carpenter or mason carry them into a successful realization? We think not, for such men, however excellent their workmanship may be, cannot be supposed to sympathize with your more refined notions of domestic elegance and comfort. They must, to a certain extent, realize them, but they cannot understand the *sentiment* which should pervade a design, and are content to copy and imitate, instead of composing and adapting according to the necessities of the problem laid before them.

The planning of a country house is something so peculiar and intricate, and demands careful study of so many outlying considerations, that none but an architect can do it justice. In a city house, to produce a merely respectable work, perhaps less judgment is required, as the process of design must be more or less conventional, and a certain degree of sameness is unavoidable, the same laws and requirements holding good, to a large extent, in all cases. Each house must stand on a fixed street line, and the general shape and arrangement must be somewhat similar. For the most part, it seems that the only room for the architect to display his originality is in elaborating his façade; and the restrictions of his street line, his twenty-five feet front, the city ordinances, and the conventionality of his plan, must act as a great check upon liberty of design. The only way in which he can vary the external appearance of his house from that of his neighbor, is in height of walls and stories, in material, and the detailed treatment of the uniform requirements. And even this variety must be restricted by the necessity of so harmonizing the façade with those in its neighborhood, as to prevent lines of one character, though good in themselves, from being nullified or injured by lines of another character, equally good, which may exist in proximity.

We do not mean to assert that all the buildings in a block should be uniform in all particulars, for irregularity is one of the chief beauties of architecture; but we do mean to say that one building should not be erected without some regard to harmony with those in the neighborhood, any more than a country house should be built in a style at variance with the character of surrounding scenery. To illustrate this idea with respect to harmonious city architecture, we would refer the reader to Design No. 30.

In the country, however, we are not restrained by any of these laws, but the field for design is as boundless as the variety of nature; and so is it not in bad taste to build in the country, on some choice, picturesque, or beautiful spot, a house thoroughly adapted to the city in all its details? Yet this is the most popular mode of country building. The vignette on Design No. 18, shows somewhat of this tendency, except that the roofs are usually flat, and that there are five windows in front. The interior corresponds exactly with that of a city house; having one large room with sliding doors, and two windows at either end. These, with the door, quite overload the front, and give to it an unpleasant aspect of formality. There is an obvious necessity for two windows in a city house, there being no other access for light; but here, where side windows are always added, giving twice the light that is obtained in a city drawing room, the rooms become crowded with useless windows, which give ready access to an overplus of cold in winter and heat in summer; and, as if to render the whole thing more absurd, many of these unnecessary openings are covered all the year round with blinds. No good reasons can be assigned for such concessions to fashion, and nothing can justify the conversion of a quiet rural retreat into a formal town-house. That others have done so, and continue to do so, is no excuse. From their folly let us learn wisdom.

The designs contained in this work are not intended for model houses, to be copied for all localities, but simply to show how important it is to have an original design adapted to the peculiarities of site, and how entirely erroneous it is to stereotype houses, all over the country, as has been the custom. Having selected your architect, let him visit the proposed site, that with careful study he may discover all its natural advantages, its exposures, its views, its facilities for drainage, &c., as also the disadvantages with which he must contend. Make him acquainted with your general wants, the height of your ceilings, the size and number of your rooms, and what other little details you may wish to have carried out; but the main arrangement, both inside and out, you will do well to leave wholly to him. This done, he will make you a sketch, embodying an architectural interpretation or modification of your ideas, and submit it for your approval and examination. Then, all further alterations and details of plan which may be desired being thoroughly understood by both parties, the proper working drawings will be made, subject to all the conditions of the amended design, careful specifications and contracts will be drawn up, and the whole submitted to the competition of several contractors, all of whom are known to be responsible. Thus the cheapest, readiest, and most effectual means of putting your intentions into execution will be obtained. During the progress of the work, in addition to these working drawings, consisting of the floor plans and elevations, the architect will furnish enlarged detail drawings, showing sections of external mouldings, &c., together with the internal members not seen on the other working drawings, and what other constructive explanations may be needed. That the true intent and meaning of the design may be carried out, it is essential that the architect should superintend the construction. He should visit the building during its erection, and explain the designs, and render the contractor all necessary architectural information.

Paul Schulze del.

DESIGN Nº 1.

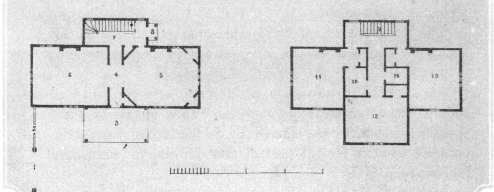

DESIGN No. 1.

THIS design may serve the double purpose of a Gate Lodge and Farm House, though the drawing was rather intended for the former, and to represent an entrance to grounds on which we propose to erect a mansion.

The architecture is of simple character, suitable for the adjunct of a neat and spacious villa, yet sufficiently pretentious to prepare us for yet greater elegance as we proceed.

There are but two rooms on the first floor—the one a kitchen, and the other a sitting room or parlor. These two rooms, being opposite each other, are entered by folding doors, which when open communicate through the hall, thus throwing the entire floor into one suite.

The stairs, it will be observed, are located in such a manner as to leave the main hall unobstructed, thus removing the thoroughfare from the body of the house ; which object is also facilitated by a rear entrance on first floor and basement.

The second floor is very spacious, being much larger than the first on account of its projection over the entrance porch. By this means we have an additional chamber, making three in all each provided with a closet. On the right is a large linen closet, while on the left is placed what may be deemed an unusual and perhaps unnecessary convenience for a gate lodge—a bath room. Certainly there is the truest and most humane economy in providing servants and all those under our protection with the means of enjoying the great blessing of cleanliness, which is the first advance to civilization, refinement, and self-respect.

The windows of this second story are somewhat elevated, but are so placed to avoid cutting through the wall plate, or horizontal beam on which the roof rests, thereby weakening the building and increasing the expense.

With reference to Gate Lodges it may be remarked, that for places of moderate size such an appendage is pretentious and inappropriate. Too frequently we meet with an ostentatious lodge standing but a few paces from a modest dwelling, displaying a singular disregard of the obvious proprieties of life, without the excuse of usefulness. When the domain is extensive, and the residence properly located at a distance from the highway, an entrance lodge is highly appropriate and necessary, not only as a home for the gardener or farmer, where one of the family may always be in readiness to open and close the gates on the arrival of carriages, but as a protection to the place from the trespass of improper persons. Lodges may not be considered objectionable features when attached to places situated near the road, if the grounds are so planned and planted as to afford a proper amount of retirement from observation, and through the contrivance of the landscape gardening are made to appear more ample than they are. It is proposed to presently treat this subject of artificial perspective more at large.

Gate Lodges, as well as all other outbuildings, should, in their architectural treatment, partake somewhat of the style of the dwellings to which they are subordinate, but should in all cases be of a much simpler and perhaps of a more rustic character, as is befitting their modest office in the duties of household hospitality.

Estimate.—A Gate Lodge of this character could be built, under favorable circumstances, for from $800 to $1,000.*

* The following estimates include simply the mason's and carpenter's contracts.

Paul Schulze del.

DESIGN Nº 2.

DESIGN No. 2.

THE architect, in the discharge of his duties, is called upon to perform many severe tasks, but none more arduous than that of remodelling a country house, where he has to contend with the blunders and conventional distortions of "carpenters' architecture," to develop harmony out of discord, beauty out of ugliness, elegance out of the commonplace. Consider, reader, how you would appal an artist of recognised ability by applying to him to finish a picture commenced by one who had no more exalted idea of art than what might be acquired in the æsthetic meditations of house and sign painting; how you would shock a Hosmer or Powers by presenting for the finishing touches of their delicate chisels some rude sculpture attempted by an ordinary stonecutter. Would not the enthusiastic devotee of art wonder at your applying to such a source at the first, and still more when you would have him remodel and give to the ill-used marble character and expression? Would he not, with all the eloquence inspired by his profession, remonstrate against your course in employing at the outset so inferior an artist, and earnestly set forth the difficulty of overcoming the many radical errors of the inexperienced tyro? Would he not justly fear the injury he might do his own reputation by undertaking it at all? Yet every day do we see men of wealth, and sometimes of intelligence, applying to ignorant builders, self-styled architects, to furnish designs for cottages, villas, or even mansions of great pretension.

For in that very worthy class of mechanics, some one may be found in every town, whose ambition or conceit has so led him astray from his true path, that we find him rushing in where artists might fear to tread, and leaving such traces of his folly as render the whole neighborhood hideous with the whims of his untutored imagination. He may "draught a plan" which on paper will deceive the eye of the client, and actually persuade him into the delusion that, as it is the composition of a " practical man," it will appear well when erected. For many have thus unfortunately built in haste, and repented at leisure.

The usual resort in such cases, after the building is spoiled, is to apply to an architect of recognized ability to remodel the work. With perplexed brain the professional man sets about his expensive and difficult task of correcting that which, had it in the outset been properly done, would have saved both himself and the owner much vexation and annoyance.

Design No. 2 represents a cottage which the author remodelled for Dr. C. W. Ballard, at Noroton Darien, Conn. The original structure, which is shown in the vignette at the left, was purchased by its present owner of a farmer, and is a good specimen of the small farm houses or cottages of Connecticut. Devoid of beauty, grace, or expression, pinched and contracted in all its features, placed usually in the most unattractive spot, directly on the road, with a formal avenue of cherry trees leading up to the door. These structures are indefinitely multiplied in the rural districts, and are the natural homes of a thrifty and enterprising, but unimaginative, tasteless, and perhaps overworked people.

The ceilings are low, and the rooms small, crooked, and without ventilation ; green wooden shutters *adorn* the windows, and the outer walls, if painted at all, are sure to be of a staring white or a brilliant red; yet within the shadow of the humblest of these cottages have been born and reared some of the most distinguished men of our history. Perhaps there still exist, under such unpromising shelter, many " hands which the rod of empire might have swayed." Let it be our task to surround them with such refining influences as will render them better fitted for the higher and nobler life, and will smooth for them the upward path. Let us, in short, give them *homes* which may refine and elevate as well as shelter.

Yet, when a man of true taste and refinement comes in possession of so unpromising a subject as this, our drawing, we think, proves that with no considerable expense, effects of a striking and elegant nature may be produced, and the wholly unprepossessing building, under proper hands, be made comparatively a model of beauty no less than of convenience.

The vignette on the right represents an ornamental well curb, and shows how that appendage, ordinarily so awkward and ungainly, may be made a pleasing feature of the grounds, and an earnest of the elegant hospitality of the residence to which it is attached. The well, ever grateful in its associations with memories of dripping coolness, in the parched summer time, of mid-day repose, and of many an office of friendship in the presenting of the cup of cold water to the weary traveller, should always be adorned with the most affectionate fancies at our command.

Paul Schulze, del.

DESIGN Nº 3.

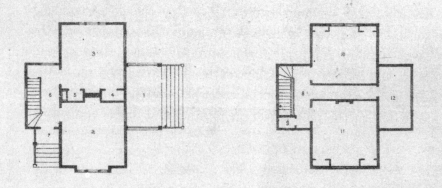

DESIGN No. 3.

It is often imagined by those who desire to build economically, that beauty is an extravagance in which they cannot indulge, and therefore that a cheap cottage can necessarily have no pretensions to elegance, and barely suffice for the comfort and shelter of its occupants: no higher aim is attempted. This error arises from the false but prevalent idea that beauty and grace are entirely extraneous considerations, rather matters of ornament than proportion and symmetry of parts. For this reason many small houses, whose owners wish to render them objects of taste, are loaded down with unmeaning and expensive decorations, or so frittered away with cheap and ready expedients of boards sawn, cut, planed, and otherwise tortured into utter uselessness and absurdity, that the entire building becomes subordinate to its appendages, and the arrangement of its important masses is entirely lost sight of.

When the architect is called upon to design a very cheap building, he must be content to express his art in the fitness and proportion of all its parts; he must combine beauty with the strictest utility. Thus in this design, which was prepared for a gentleman in Connecticut, we have availed ourselves of the necessity of providing an artificial shade by simply projecting the eaves; this at once gives to the cottage a pleasant expression of shelter. The windows naturally require more protection from the sun and rain than the walls, and, therefore, over these the eaves are extended one foot more than elsewhere, and in consequence of this extra projection require brackets for support.

The veranda in our climate has become a national feature, and is certainly a most useful as well as ornamental appendage to a house. In this particular instance its introduction adds much to the beauty and comfort of the cottage. An ornamental rail protects its sides, while strong timber brackets assist in supporting the superincumbent weight.

The bay window, always a charming feature, blends harmoniously with the design, and, by its intervention, breaks up a formal regularity of wall, both outside and in. Though of small dimensions, it not only materially enlarges the *actual* size of the room to which it is attached, but apparently, through the perspective effect always produced by an outward break of this kind, opens a much larger space within than it really does.

These then, it will be observed, are matters of practical utility in protection, construction, and comfort, and the only feature that seems superfluous is the ornament on the roof. This, it is granted, according to strict rules of economy, might be omitted, for there can be no other than an æsthetical use attributed to it, especially as the chimney, from its central position, has the effect of relieving the roof and sustaining the soaring tendency of the lines; still, to project a pattern like this against the sky on any ridge, certainly gives a very desirable and emphatic quality of crispiness to the design.

The first floor is arranged with sitting and dining rooms; the latter having two closets, one for china, and the other containing a dumb waiter which communicates with the kitchen below. The second floor comprises three good bedrooms and a linen closet. This story, for purposes of economy, is low, the side walls being six feet high to the roof, whence the ceiling starts at an angle, somewhat less than that of the roof, making the ceiling flatter and forming an air space between it and the roof, which protects the rooms from external changes of atmosphere. This object is also facilitated by the ceiling being deafened, thus making these rooms as comfortable as if they had an entire story over them.

It will be seen by this that we contrive to obviate that great objection commonly entertained against houses of a story and a half in height, that the bedrooms are like ovens in summer, and like refrigerators at other seasons. We would take advantage of this opportunity strongly to recommend the use of deafening in all floors; as it is not only serviceable in preventing the passage of sound from one room to another, but in binding the floors together and rendering them stiffer and more solid. Little expenditures like these, judiciously made, will never be regretted when the house is finished, since they soon pay for themselves in a saving of fuel, to say nothing of the protection they give from dampness, heat, and cold.

Estimate.—This design, though on a somewhat larger scale,

was built for John W. Shedden, Esq., on the Morris and Essex Railroad, about one mile beyond South Orange, N. J. With an arrangement as shown, it would cost from $800 to $1,000, being of about the same dimensions as design No. 1.

Paul Schulze del.

DESIGN Nº 4.

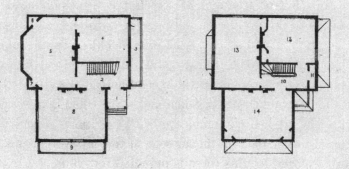

DESIGN No. 4.

This design is for a cheap cottage, with commodious accommodations, and of pleasing external appearance, uniting economy and convenience. It was intended for a village lot in Stamford, Conn., of 75 feet frontage, of which the principal façade of the house was to occupy 25 feet, giving an equal space on either side. The house is of two stories, with a basement and attic, affording a spacious drawing room, library, and dining room on the first floor, with six large chambers on the second and in the attic. The bedrooms for servants, with kitchen and store cellars, are in the basement. The kitchen communicates with the dining room by a dumb waiter, through one of the closets in the latter apartment. The opposite closet in this room is intended for china and table linen A large linen closet is shown on the second story. Instead of veran-

das we have adopted terraces with canopy roofs over them, supported by brackets, which are much more economical than posts
or columns, though perhaps not as commodious. The entrance
porch, which is at the side, has a balcony over it, with access
from the second story hall.

One peculiarity of this design is the truncated or "gambrel"
roof, used to give space to the upper rooms, and to lessen the
apparent height of the structure, which, if composed of three entire stories, would be too lofty for the amount of ground it occupies. This expedient also gives a pleasing variety to the lines of the
roof, a feature usually so bare of interest. This differs from the
common "gambrel" roof of New England farm houses and home-
steads, in the projection of the eaves, and in the truncation of the
gable ends, which makes a hipped roof of the upper slope, giving
to the general outline a pleasant resemblance to the rustic hay-
rick, and affording a more immediate shelter to the gable windows
from the sun and rain. The decorated barge boards at the eaves
produce shadows, relieve the walls, and serve as a protection to the
sides of the house, thus forming a useful and ornamental appendage, often cheaper than brackets. The ballustrades of perforated
plank, around the balconies and terraces, partake of the style of
the house, corresponding with the barge boards, and contributing
to the harmony of the design.

One great advantage architects possess in this country is the
strong contrast of light and shade produced by our clear atmosphere, which assists materially in producing good effects in building. The introduction of irregularities, such as projections of
roofs, canopies, verandas, and bay windows, together with the in-
tersections of gables, dormers, and the height of chimneys, serve to
break up the bare formality of the usual barn-like outline, and to
obtain the ever varying sentiment and expression which the

great Architect never fails to give to all his rocks and hills. Light and shade are the happiest instruments of design, and most easily procured in our climate, and are ever ready to give new life and spirit to forms properly managed for their play. The repetition of the perforated barge boards in shadow against the walls, ever making new interpretaions of its patterns, shows how tenderly and delicately nature assists the sympathetic architect.

In cities, where the great value of land almost precludes the designer from availing himself of opposing masses of light and shade, which can be produced in emphasis only by costly irregularities of plan, and large reëntering angles of outer walls, it seems necessary to resort to some other expedient where delicacy of line is not considered a sufficient substitute for the more massive effects of *chiaro-oscuro*. The luxurious and sensuous Mahometans, not content with the more serious and sober habits of the North in design, not only were in the habit of breaking their sky lines with pierced parapets and lily patterns, with swelling domes, with endless pinnacles and fantastic minarets, to a degree never thought of elsewhere, but availed themselves of strong and vivid contrasts of bright colors. It would be well for us to take a lesson from the Eastern nations in this respect, and while we repudiate perhaps, as undignified, any complete adaptation of their endless fancies of form, to study their picturesque use of external colors, and let the walls of our cities assume new life and meaning by contrasting tints of various bricks and stones, and the introduction of brilliant tiles and slates of different quarries. This source of design, if used with discretion in our Metropolitan structures, would effect the happiest results, and preserve their architecture from inanity and insipidity. But in the country, where growth of shapes and forms is unchecked by any considerations of economy of space, it seems almost superfluous to use decorative external color to any very great extent, certainly, we think, never for its own sake, as in the town; but so far as it may serve to protect wooden surfaces, to assist in giving expression to form, and to harmonize masses with the nature around, its employment is of great value. It is, then, important to know by what rule we are to be governed in the use of colors under these circumstances. It is evident that the general tint covering the plain surface of a small house surrounded by trees, should be light and cheerful, warm in its tone, and of a neutral rather than positive character, as the latter very readily harmonizes with nature. But do not fall into the opposite extreme, and paint your house white, which is no color at all, always cold and glaring, and makes an ugly *spot* in any landscape; we find nothing there to warrant so forcible an intrusion. A white building might not be so objectionable in the city, where we have no nature to assimilate to and work with; but in the country nothing but snow and chalk cliffs are white, and these put out the eyes by their intensity. Choose, then, any of the hundred soft, neutral tints which may afford to your house the cheerfulness or dignity it may require. These are to be determined especially by its location and size. A house of large and commanding proportions, occupying a conspicuous position in the scenery, would present a ludicrous appearance if painted a light color; while one of smaller size, subordinate to its natural surroundings, and well shaded by trees, would, if painted dark, give an impression of gloom.

Having selected the general tint, the trimmings should be of a darker shade of the same, or a deeper color, to give them prominence, and assist in bringing out the design. The roof, when not covered with slate, should resemble it somewhat in color, and the window blinds, when used at all, should be darker even than the window dressings, and should assimilate in color to the general tone of the house.

It is always advisable to consult the architect as to his views in this matter of color, since an improper application of paint might quite nullify the effect of his design, and render that ridiculous which was intended to be dignified, small which was intended to appear large, and obtrusive which was intended to be modest and retiring.

By a judicious subordination of various tints, many errors and incongruities of style may be lessened or quite concealed, and the good points of design be properly emphasized and made to assume a worthy prominence in the composition.

Estimate.—This design would cost, under favorable circumstances, about $3,000.

Paul Schulze, del.

DESIGN Nº 5.

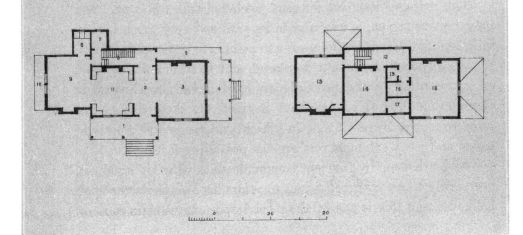

DESIGN No. 5.

THIS cottage, designed for some secluded valley in a wild and mountainous region, is irregular in its plan and very much broken in its sky lines, in order the nearer to assimilate to the character of the scenery amidst which it is placed, and to form a natural part of it, according to the principle we have already touched upon. Considering these things, we have instinctively adopted some motives from the Swiss Chalet, in which galleries, very projecting eaves, and great extent of roof are the prevailing features.

A gentleman, by frequent communications with his architect, necessarily to a very great extent imprints his own character upon his house, and this is one of the most important æsthetic ends of the art, and proves how possible it is to express in a manner even the most delicate idiosyncracies of human character. It is the duty of the architect, studying the desires and needs of his client, carefully to manage the design in all its parts, so as to fit into and harmonize with the lives to be spent under its roof.

Thus a house of this kind, we think, will at once impress the beholder with the conviction that it is the habitation of a gentleman of small family and limited means, yet possessing education and refinement, and an appreciation so delicate for the scenery amidst which he lives that he would have his very dwelling-place sympathize with it, and be a fit companion for its rocky undulations and its forests of pine and hemlock.

The library, occupying the central portion of the house, shows that this is his favorite room, from which he can easily approach his drawing room on the one side or his dining room on the other. Evidently he is rather a man of nice literary taste than a close student, for this apartment is too liable to intrusion and household noise to serve the purposes of a study, strictly so considered. The size of his drawing room indicates his fondness for society, and the arrangement of the folding doors, by which the entire first floor may be thrown into one apartment, gives evidence of generous hospitality and large social qualities.

The dining room opens into a spacious butler's pantry, containing a dresser for table linen and china, also a sink with hot and cold water, and a dumb waiter communicating with a similar pantry below, connected with the kitchen. Over this pantry, in the second story, a bath room might be made; but none is here introduced on account of the expense. The dining room and kitchen chimney is placed partly outside to give more room within, at the same time relieving the external plainness and forming one of the architectural features of the house.

The balcony from the dining room window forms a shelter over the kitchen door, which, on account of the descent of the grade in this direction, is entirely above ground, making a fine, light, and dry kitchen, connecting with the store cellars and servants' apartments, also on this floor.

A kitchen arranged in this manner is better than one on the same level with the dining room, as in the latter case the erection of an additional building is necessary, increasing the expense, and being inconvenient by reason of the distance to the store cellars. By this arrangement also, the servants have apartments so removed that they are not brought into immediate contact with the family; and if the floor is deafened the noise and disagreeable odors from the kitchen are more effectually excluded from the main house. The admirable plan now generally in use, for dumb waiters, renders them noiseless, and obviates entirely the necessity of passing up and down stairs for each article required. When possible, it is well to have the dumb waiter communicating between the chamber floors and kitchen, or laundry, to carry clean or soiled linen, &c.; this arrangement renders back or servants' staircases almost unnecessary.

The bedrooms on the second story have each a closet (with another in the hall for linen), and fireplaces, with a studied arrangement for the furniture, a matter too often neglected in planning a house. Nothing is more common than to see sleeping apartments so constructed that no place is left for a bed without interfering with a door, window or fireplace, no place in the dining room for a sideboard, no place in the drawing room for a piano or sofa, no place in the library for bookcases, and no place in the dressing room for a toilet table.

This also proves the danger of altering an architect's design without his consent, since there are always certain meanings and

intentions for every detail, however trifling, obvious to none but
the originator. To change a door or window, therefore, is very
apt to interfere with some internal or external feature of the
design. If the architect is consulted, he can usually devise a way
to carry out any alteration without interfering with the arrangements of the general plan.

Estimate.—A building like this could be erected for about
$2,500.

Paul Schulze del.

DESIGN N° 6.

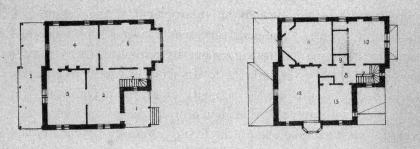

DESIGN No. 6.

FIRST FLOOR PLAN.	SECOND FLOOR PLAN.
1. Veranda.	7. Staircase.
2. Hall, 13 × 19.	8. Hall.
3. Drawing Room, 15 × 19.	9. Linen Closet.
4. Library, 15 × 19.	10. Bedroom, 15 × 19.
5. Veranda.	11. Do. 15 × 19.
6. Dining Room, 15 × 22.	12. Do. 15 × 19.
7. Staircase.	13. Do. 12 × 13.

WE recommend this design, not only for the agreeable and elegant effects of its exterior, but also for its economical and simple yet commodious arrangements within. The entrance porch, which is apparently distinct, acts as an enlargement of the veranda, of which it is a part. The hall serves as a large sitting room, and communicates with the drawing room by folding doors, while the stairs, which ascend through the tower, from basement to attic, are so secluded, as to obviate the necessity of a private staircase.

It must be admitted that to enter at once into a large hall, treated somewhat like one of the living rooms of the house, and perhaps with a wood fire blazing cheerfully on one side in a wide open chimney, gives to the stranger the impression of generous hospitality and cordial greeting, as if the house itself at once had received him into its arms. This is frequent in England.

The dining room has a bay window, and communicates with the library by folding doors. The second story has a linen closet and four good bedrooms, and the attic has similar rooms. The windows throughout have deep embrasures and broad sills, which are 15 inches from the floor. With cushions, these form convenient and pleasant seats, and assist in furnishing the room.

The veranda, it will be observed, is rather limited, yet as a greater portion is on the east side of the house, it is in the shade the most of the day. It should always be remembered that where there is but one veranda it should be placed on the shady side of the house. Great mistakes are often made in painting the veranda roof a light color, for the purpose of coolness. But actually the effect is directly the reverse, the light tones reflecting the heat into the chamber windows. It is true that the roof is thus left cool, but it is no advantage, since if the rooms within are hot we care little how cool the veranda roof may be. The roof here, as over all parts of the house, is of dark slate, a material especially harmonious with brick or stone houses. When slate is used, however, sufficient steepness should be obtained to shed the water, while flat roofs should be covered with metal. The main roof here has, on account of its steepness, no gutter at the cornice, as the water is nearly all collected from the flat on top, in gutters at the curb of the roof. The objection often holds good, against towers arranged like the one in our design, that the snow will lodge between it and the main roof, and cause leakage. But by reference to the plan it will be seen that, in order to give entrance to the attic, this space must be filled up by a passage, the roof of which, not shown in this perspective, prevents such a lodging place. Expedients of this kind should always be resorted to in our climate, since picturesque vallies or internal angles of this kind are apt to leak.

We would take advantage of this opportunity to advise the application of some distinctive name to every detached country house, however small, since it cannot be distinguished by a number, as in town. The name should, of course, be suggestive of some fact connected with the house, its owner, or its location, and should be original, or at least not copied from any in the vicinity.

We would offer, as names not yet become common among us, the following taken from country seats in England, which may serve as suggestions:

Arborfield,	Brook Cottage,	Elmwood,	Highmont,
Ashhill,	Brookvale,	Fern Hill,	Ivy Cottage,
Ashfield,	Brookfield,	Fern Cottage,	Ivy Hill,
Ashridge,	Brook Hill,	Forest Hill,	Laurel Cottage,
Ashdale,	Brookwood,	Glen Villa,	Lawn Cottage,
Bayfield,	Blithefield,	Glenfield,	Longwood,
Bayswater,	Chestnut Cottage,	Glen Cottage,	Mayfield,
Baythorne,	Claremont,	Greenhill,	Myrtle Cottage,
Beach Cottage,	Cliff Hall,	Grove Cottage,	Melrose,
Beach Hill,	Cliff Cottage,	Grove Park,	Moss Side,
Beachside,	Crow's Nest,	Harewood,	Moss Cottage,
Beech Hill,	Cedars,	Haselwood,	Oak Bank,
Beech Land,	Clifton,	Hawthorne,	Oak Hall,
Beechwood,	Dale Park,	Hawkswood,	Oak Cottage,
Beltwood,	Daisy Bank,	Hayfield,	Oak Hill,
Berry Hill,	Doveridge,	Highwood,	Oakfield,
Birchwood,	Eaglehurst,	Highlands,	Oakwood,
Bloomfield,	Edgehill,	Holly Cottage,	Oaklands,
The Briars,	Elm Cottage,	Holly Grove,	Oatlands,
Broadlands,	Elm Grove,	Holly Hill,	Oldbrook,
Broadfield,	Elmstead,	Homewood,	Oldfield,

Oriel Cottage,	Sedgebrook,	Summerfield,	Westfield,
Raven Hill,	Sedgefield,	Sunning Hill,	Westwood,
Ravensdale,	Shelbrook,	Thorne Hill,	Willow Cottage,
Ridge Cottage,	Shoreham,	Thorne Grove,	Winfield,
Ridgwood,	Shrubhill,	Undercliff,	Woodbines,
Ringwood,	Spring Cottage,	Vine Cottage,	Woodcote,
Rosedale,	Spring Grove,	Walnut Springs,	Woodfield,
Roseland,	Spring Hill,	Walnut Grove,	Woodhill,
Roseberry,	Springwood,	Waterside,	Woodford,
Rushbrook,	Strawberry,	Wedgewood,	Woodlands,
Rockingham,	Summer Hill,	Westbrook,	Woodside,

Estimate.—This design, if built of stone, would cost about $4,500.

Paul Schulze del.

DESIGN Nº 7.

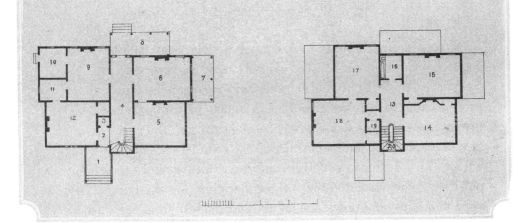

DESIGN No. 7.

FIRST FLOOR PLAN.

1. Entrance Porch, 9 × 10.
2. Vestibule.
3. Coat Closet.
4. Main Hall.
5. Library, 15 × 18.
6. Drawing Room, 15 × 20.
7. Veranda.
8. Do.
9. Kitchen, 15 × 17.
10. Sink Room, 10 × 10.
11. Butler's Pantry, 7 × 10.
12. Dining Room, 15 × 18.

SECOND STORY PLAN.

13. Hall.
14. Chamber, 13 × 18.
15. Do.   15 × 20.
16. Bath Room, 8 × 8.
17. Chamber, 15 × 17.
18. Do.   15 × 18.
19. Linen Closet.
20. Tower Staircase.

THERE seem to be two classes of people who delight in an occasional retirement to the wildest, most picturesque, and unfrequented spots; who find it necessary, at certain intervals, to approach nature, when she abandons herself to her most fantastic and savage moods; to hear her great heart beating in the midst of her grandest solitudes, and to partake of the rude fare of the abounding wilderness. The man of letters and high culture yields to this impulse with the strong desire of recuperating his intellect at the very fountains of knowledge, of freeing himself from the dust of books, and of catching new emotions and intelligible ideas from the secret spirit whispers of the "forest primeval." The man of the world, on the other hand, seeks the same scenery, weary of his routine of dissipation, to obtain a new zest for his life amidst the bounteous freshness of nature, in the fish of her wandering mountain brooks and lovely lakes, and in the wild game of the endless woodland. Mount Desert, Moosehead Lake, the Adirondacks, and the Saguenay have all in turn been the savage Meccas of pale pilgrims who have followed the adventurous trail of the Indian, the hunter, the backwoodsman, and the artist, and sought with them refreshment, consolation, health, and the pleasures of delightful novelty.

In all these places—in the wildest and most picturesque of them—we find these pilgrims, not content with a brief, homeless tarrying there, building their huts and hunting lodges, and shooting boxes, for more convenient and easier sojourn in the summer. The philosophers of Cambridge and the sportsmen of Gotham have not only, like Cowper, longed

> " for a lodge in some vast wilderness,
> Some boundless contiguity of shade,"

but have made a prophecy of their desires and set up their rude household gods in the bosom of the Adirondacks, and by the forest borders of Lake George. Sunnysides and Idlewilds and Clovernooks are arising in abundance far from the trodden paths of travel; peaceful vine-clad fortresses for protection against the raids of *enemies*, and of all the world's follies, gaities, and dissipations— strongholds of homely, hearty hospitality, where the prodigal son may go back to the bosom of nature and find her affections unchanged, and her kind indulgence the same as in the pleasant associations of his childhood.

To meet requirements of this kind, we have prepared the accompanying design, adapted equally well for a hermitage or shooting lodge. The style adopted is that usually termed the "half timber;" in which the framing is allowed to appear externally and form the prominent decorative characteristic of the structure, while between the timbers there is a filling in of brick nogging or rough cast. The effect of this method of construction is highly pleasing, the wall surface being constantly relieved by this expression of wood construction, which is not merely suggestive of strength, but actually increases the firmness of the building. Examples of this style are constantly found in England and on the Continent; it is universal; many of them date back to quite a remote antiquity. Their stability is only exceeded by their picturesqueness and venerable beauty. The traveller will remember with what quaint freaks of form and color they hang over the narrow streets of Chester and Rouen.

The chimneys in this design are carried up to an unusual height, which, with the tower and the gables rising one above the other, strongly partakes of the character of the wooded mountain scenery around, while the broad spread and irregular contour of the roofs are in sympathy with the undulating sweep of valleys and prairie lands.

As we approach this house, the first feature that attracts our attention is the porch leading to the front door. This is quite spacious, admitting the gathering of family groups under its shelter, thus taking the place of a formal veranda, and with the strength of its crossing and supporting timbers bearing its harmonious part in the general sentiment of the design. We enter the vestibule, which is separated from the main hall by an arch. This hall begins at the tower and runs to the rear of the house. The main stairs, commencing at the vestibule and ascending through the tower, afford a landing on each story up to the observatory. The dining room, which is on the left, has a china closet, and communicates with the kitchen through a large butler's pantry, which also serves as a store room. The kitchen is provided with a spacious sink room.

The second story contains four bedrooms, a bath room and linen closet.

In arranging the rooms on the principal story, we have had constant consideration of the fact that they were intended not for any such formal hospitalities as balls or *fêtes*, but rather for that internal domestic comfort, that *dolce far niente* and *abandon* which the occupant came into the wilderness to find. Here the broadcloth coat or silk dress becomes a myth, and the bachelor's cigar knows no housekeeper's tyrannical limitations.

Estimate.—This design, if built plainly, would cost about $3,000.

Paul Schulze del.

DESIGN N.º 8.

DESIGN No. 8.

THE accompanying cottage, which is the residence of John R. Kearney, Esq., at Rye, N. Y., was originally as shown in the vignette at the left, but was enlarged and altered to its present appearance from plans submitted by the author. The great defects of the old house were a want of relief from monotony and absence of shadows. In order to obtain these results in the altered design, the roofs were extended, and the projecting gable thrown up at the long unbroken side, while the little one-story addition served to create an irregularity upon the ground. The ornament upon the eaves was removed and placed upon the ridge, the chimney altered in design, and the gables surmounted by finials.

The site it occupies is quite picturesque, and rocks and wildwood form the principal features of the scenery. In order to create a harmonious design, rustic work was introduced for the verandas, balconies, and supports of gables.

The vignette at the right represents a stable belonging to John Howland, Esq., at Belle Point, Darien, Conn., which was altered from an ordinary farm barn to its present appearance.

The stable itself is in the basement; the first floor is occupied by carriage house, tool house, grain and store rooms, with an apartment for a servant, and above these is the hay loft.

The feed is received in the basement through "shoots" which

are convenient to the horses. This stable is provided with two loose boxes and four stalls. These are paved with brick, the rest of the floor being of stone. There are two ventilators connecting with the lantern on the roof.

With regard to harness rooms, we would suggest that they be made larger than they usually are, and with some means of heating them to prevent the cracking of the harness by cold. Here, too, is a smoking room for gentlemen in the morning, and which may also serve as a pleasant resort for male servants in the evening.

Paul Schulze, del.

DESIGN N⁰ 9.

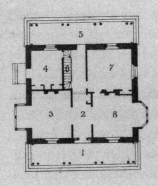

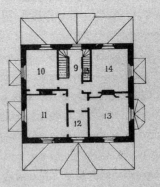

0   20   40

DESIGN No. 9.

THIS design, which is alluded to in Chapter II., was executed at Rye, N. Y., for Dr. J. H. T. Cockey. It is charmingly located, overlooking the windings of a pleasant stream through a beautiful bit of country. The grounds comprise about twenty acres, and in the centre is a natural mound, on which the house was built.

On excavating for the cellar, it was found that a few feet from the surface was a solid ledge of rock. Here was an obstacle not easily overcome, the only resort being a tedious process of blasting. The rock, however, proved of such excellent quality for building, as to obviate the necessity of quarrying elsewhere, and the sand and water being close at hand, no transportation of material was requisite. The rock foundation, also, it will be readily perceived, was far from objectionable, adding much to the stability of the walls. Hence the house is known as Rock Cottage.

In building square houses, the chimneys are usually four in number, and placed at the sides; in this design, however, the reader will notice that there are but two, and these built inside the house, in the place generally occupied by folding doors. The expense is, of course, thus decreased, and by the situation of these chimneys much of the heat is retained which would otherwise be wasted upon outside walls. Instead of the two rooms on one side, communicating with each other by folding doors, according to the usual arrangement, here, apartments on opposite sides of the hall are placed *en suite* by double doors, thus including the hall itself. These doors and the opposite bay windows have arches over their openings, so that standing in the bays we may see a succession of four of these in vista, affording thus an imposing feature to the rooms.

The dining room is slightly enlarged by being extended somewhat into the hall, while the library is made smaller to give space for removing the stairs from the passage, thus obviating the necessity of a private staircase. The second story has five good chambers, and there are also three bedrooms in the attic.

We have already had occasion to remark that regularity or formal balance of parts in strictly rural architecture is not generally desirable. But in scenery of rather a mildly beautiful than wild or picturesque character, the more symmetrical designs are often admissible and sometimes singularly appropriate, the formal and stately seats, so common among the residences of the English gentry, most abound along the broad and easy slopes of the country side, by placid lakes and quiet streams, among gently undulating grassy lawns and parks, adorned with detached clumps of elms or oaks. Though we would scarcely wish to see repeated to any extent the quaint formalities of an old-fashioned Elizabethan garden, with its thick yew-tree hedges clipped into arcades and all sorts of strange fantasies of form, with its straight alleys and long artificial vistas, yet some sort of formality is often desirable in the midst of such park-like scenery as we have described, and we are justified in borrowing the terraces, fountains, and ballustrades of the Italian villa, and the nicely trimmed hedges, neat gravel walks and strictly kept boundaries of the English country seat. With such surroundings a purely symmetrical design is often most appropriate, especially when the house is very spacious. An American village, too, with its rectangular lots on the street, seems to suggest sometimes a similar formality of treatment on a smaller scale.

But let us change the location and imagine one more pictu-resque. Though the simple and inexpensive internal arrangement of the square cottage may be retained, we shall readily perceive that a strictly symmetrical external treatment would appear mis-placed. It is usually supposed that in order to render a design picturesque, the plan must of necessity be irregular. This is a very common error; and in selecting a certain fixed plan, it is generally considered that the elevation attached to it must be ad-hered to under all circumstances. As an evidence that the adoption of such a plan does not necessarily involve a disregard of exterior agreeing with the surrounding scene, we would refer the reader to Design No. 15. This certainly has the appearance of an entirely different arrangement. But, on close examination, it will be found that not only the general disposition of rooms, but every door and window, with the single exception of an alteration of the bay, corresponds precisely in plan with the present design; whereas the exterior only is altered to suit a more picturesque style of country, by simply breaking the lines of the roof, and by certain contrivances of detail, giving the whole an entirely different aspect, and adapting it thoroughly to its new condition of site.

Estimate.—This design was built by contract for $4,500.

Paul Schulze, del.

DESIGN, Nº 10.

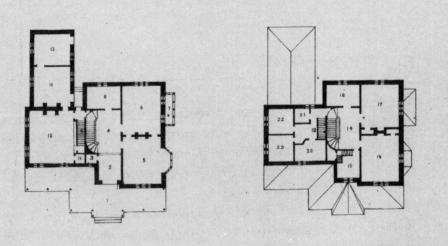

0   20   40

DESIGN No. 10.

FIRST FLOOR PLAN.	SECOND FLOOR PLAN.
1. Veranda.	14. Hall, 8 × 16.
2. Vestibule, 9 × 10.	15. Chamber, 9 × 9.
3. Coat Closet.	16. Do. 15 × 17.
4. Hall, 9 × 16.	17. Do. 15 × 17.
5. Drawing Room, 19 × 19.	18. Do. 9 × 13.
6. Library, 15 × 19.	19. Hall.
7. Green House.	20. Bath Room, 13 × 19.
8. Sewing Room, 9 × 13.	21. Linen Closet, 6 × 6.
9. Servants' Staircase.	22. Bedroom, 10 × 10.
10. Dining Room, 19 × 20.	23. Do. 10 × 10.
11. China Closet.	
12. Kitchen, 15 × 16.	
13. Woodshed, 12 × 16.	

SUCH picturesqueness and diversity of feature, as characterize the treatment of this little villa, are well adapted for association with the wild, romantic scenery of many parts of our country, especially on those abrupt and rugged slopes so common along the banks of the Hudson.

This structure, which was designed as a residence for J. D. Bedford, Esq., is situated on one of these slopes, at Nyack.

Its style is strictly Tudor, the same so frequent in those choice localities among the lakes and mountain districts of England.

The variety of its skylines, obtained by a careful composition of clustered chimneys, gabled roofs and pointed finials, is in harmony with the rugged character of the scenery around it; while its broad veranda, bay window, and greenhouse serve to assist its irregularity of outline on the ground, and to relieve the monotony of formal and unsympathizing walls. The little gable at the right breaks up and relieves the long extent of cornice on that façade, and the chimney produces the same effect upon the ridge. The pyramidal form of the group is effected by the towering of the observatory in its central position, and the whole produces in the general picture some resemblance to the peculiar features of the landscape itself. The design is chiefly commendable for its convenience and its proper conformity with its immediate surroundings.

Another composition of equal merit, yet wholly different in architectural character, may be found in Design No. 29. Here may be seen an example of the horizontal tendency of those classic structures whose representations awaken so many pleasing memories in the mind of one who has traversed the sunny plains of Italy; but agreeable as they may be in a level region, a due attention to fitness admonishes us that an edifice designed after their manner, would be quite inappropriate in the more rugged portions of our country. And why is this? We reply that an article of apparel, which is highly becoming to one person, proves frequently quite the reverse to another, and thus, in order to be tastefully attired, one must take into consideration form, complexion, and features, and then select garments of a corresponding color and shape. This, though a homely comparison, is precisely analogous to the immediate question; a building, therefore, to be an object of art, should conform in shape, color, and feature with the country around. Thus the level, unbroken lines of the Italian villa, so decidedly in harmony with the smooth, placid character of its native land, would be as greatly out of place amid the wild, imposing grandeur of the Catskills, as would the rude beauty of the Gothic on the fair plains of Italy.

The interior of this building is more unique than extensive. The entrance, which is in the tower, opens into a spacious vestibule, provided with a coat closet, and is separated from the main hall by an arch, where folding doors may be placed in winter. The hall is also of good size, the staircase being in an alcove at the side, under which a sofa may be properly placed. The first apartment at the right is the drawing room, which has a bay window, and connects with the library by doors on either side of the fireplace: sliding doors might be introduced and the rooms thrown together at pleasure. The library has sufficient space for books, and is connected with a small greenhouse on the south side, which may be heated in winter by simply opening the glass doors by which it communicates with the library. It is protected from external cold by double glazed sashes: the floor and ceiling being deafened and the panels backed with brick. At the end of the hall is a small room, which may serve as a sewing or smoking room, or private office. The dining room and kitchen occupy the wing, which has its ceiling lower than the main part of the house; an arrangement peculiar, perhaps, but according with the taste of the owner. The upper portion of this wing is occupied by two bedrooms, a linen closet, and bath room, while there are four good chambers in the main house.

The main hall is lighted from above, and the observatory stairs, commencing at the second floor, ascend to the third and fourth stories of the tower, from whence is obtained a fine view in all directions.

Estimate.—We believe the estimates on this design were $3,500.

Paul Schulze del.

DESIGN № 11.

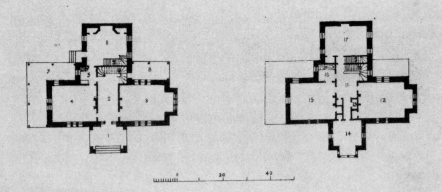

DESIGN No. 11.

NOTWITHSTANDING the general prosperity of our country and the rapidity and ease of acquiring wealth, yet in the midst of the fluctuations of commercial life, there is a constant liability to serious loss, if not entire reverses of fortune. It is sad to think that our own firesides, though far removed from the immediate bustle and keen anxieties of the exchange, are ever sensitive to the mismanagements or misfortunes of a single venture on the dangerous ocean of trade. By these, many families are driven from their luxurious mansions in the town to less pretending homes in the country. These families, thus prostrated by the changes of a day, reared in the midst of the refinements of luxurious ease, and surrounded by the golden opportunities of wealth, have, perhaps, under these impulses, so shaped their minds and manners as to have become ornaments in the circles where they were known. Such people are, of all others, equal to an emergency of this kind. They often find that adversity is not without its sweet uses. Knowing that they must, if they remain in the town, assume an inferior position, and one beneath their merits, they will turn to the country as affording a congenial home. Here, with true taste and sound judgment, they will build a cottage, which, though small in dimensions, will be complete in all its parts. In such a home, with the qualifications in themselves for making it happy, they will find, probably, a calm content unknown in the giddy turmoil of fashion, and a consolation full of gentleness and peace. Other associations, dear as those of old, will cluster around them, and they will find, as in the touching description of "the wife" in Irving's Sketch Book, that they have no desire to return to the noise and bustle, the whirl and excitement of a life in town.

Everything about such a house must be truly refined and chaste, with every convenience that comfort demands, and without any superfluities. The interior must be suggestive of the refinement of the occupants, not necessarily ornamental or showy, but in every respect tasteful and elegant. It is with such views that we have prepared the accompanying design.

The entrance porch is in character with the rest of the house, strong and substantial, and is embowered with ivy, which climbs up its columns and crowns its arches. The main stairs are at the end of the hall, which is thus left wide and unobstructed, and ready for all those uses of household pleasure which such a feature is sure to possess. The library has a bay window, and the dining room communicates with the kitchen by a butler's pantry. The kitchen has a private stairway and large closets. In the second story are four bedrooms, bath room, and linen closet, and in the attic, rooms for servants.

It is not uncommon to find in country houses one or more rooms from which the family are excluded save on rare occasions, and which are kept only for the entertainment of guests.

We have here supposed a residence for a family of refinement; and whatever is equal to its wants should certainly suffice for those of its guests. It will, then, be borne in mind that genuine hospitality does not consist in the provision, for guests, of luxuries denied ourselves. We have, therefore, omitted from this design everything superfluous. The drawing room proper is the first apartment we discard, it being one which always occupies a larger amount of space than is balanced by its actual usefulness in the household.

The ordinary objection to using a dining room for the purposes of family gatherings, is that it must necessarily be occupied by the servants after meals, for removing the service and "tidying up" generally. Much of this, however, may be obviated by the provision of a butler's pantry, and thus the dining room and hall may be used as sitting rooms, while the library remains for literary purposes.

The great want of small houses at moderate rents, and in respectable quarters of our cities, obliges many of limited means to seek homes in the country. If the custom of living on flats or floors were introduced in our country, this rural desire would be subdued, as in France; but while the old English maxim remains true of us, " every man's house is his castle," flats must be associated only with the lowest class of tenement houses. With the Anglo-Saxon, home and the family fireside are sacred, and in no small degree it is to this influence we owe our love of truth and virtue. Domestic qualities are almost unknown in France, and as a natural consequence the virtues we so much admire are held in low esteem.

It is not too much to say that every man owes it to himself, no less than his family, to provide a home; a spot around which he may gather his dear ones for counsel and instruction. Such a home is incomplete without one apartment, too often little regarded, which is a library. We would enlarge on this subject, which we deem so important, but consider it advisable rather to quote the language of a distinguished writer of the day, with which we close this chapter.

"We form judgments of men from little things about their house, of which the owner, perhaps, never thinks. In earlier years, when travelling in the West, where taverns were either scarce or, in some places, unknown, and every settler's house was a house of 'Entertainment,' it was a matter of some importance and some experience to select wisely where you would put up. And we always looked for flowers. If there were no trees for shade, no patch of flowers in the yard, we were suspicious of the place. But, no matter how rude the cabin, or rough the surroundings, if we saw that the window held a little trough for flowers, and that some vines twined about strings let down from the eaves, we were confident that there was some taste and carefulness in the log cabin. In a new country, where people have to tug for a living, no one will take the trouble to rear flowers, unless the love of them is pretty strong; and this taste blossoming out of plain and uncultivated people is, itself, like a clump of harebells growing out of the seams of a rock. We were seldom misled. A patch of flowers came to signify kind people, clean beds, and good bread.

"But, other signs are more significant in other states of society. Flowers about a rich man's house may signify only that he has a good gardener, or that he has refined neighbors and does what he sees them do.

"But men are not accustomed to buy *books* unless they want

them. If, on visiting the dwelling of a man of slender means, I find the reason why he has cheap carpets, and very plain furniture, to be that he may purchase books, he rises at once in my esteem. Books are not made for furniture, but there is nothing else that so beautifully furnishes a house. The plainest row of books that cloth or paper ever covered is more significant of refinement than the most elaborately carved *étagère*, or sideboard.

"Give me a house furnished with books rather than furniture! Both, if you can, but books at any rate! To spend several days in a friend's house, and hunger for something to read, while you are treading on costly carpets, and sitting upon luxurious chairs, and sleeping upon down, is as if one were bribing your body for the sake of cheating your mind.

"Is it not pitiable to see a man growing rich, and beginning to augment the comforts of home, and lavishing money on ostentatious upholstery, upon the table, upon everything but what the soul needs?

"We know of many and many a rich man's house where it would not be safe to ask for the commonest English classics. A few garish annuals on the table, a few pictorial monstrosities, together with the stock religious books of his "persuasion," and that is all! No range of poets, no essayists, no selection of historians, no travels or biographies, no select fictions, or curious legendary lore; but, then, the walls have paper on which cost three dollars a roll, and the floors have carpets that cost four dollars a yard! Books are the windows through which the soul looks out. A house without books is like a room without windows. No man has a right to bring up his children without surrounding them with books, if he has the means to buy them. It is a wrong to his family. He cheats them! Children learn to read by being in the presence of books. The love of knowledge comes with reading and grows upon it. And the love of knowledge, in a young mind, is almost a warrant against the inferior excitement of passions and vices.

"Let us pity these poor rich men who live barrenly in great, bookless houses! Let us congratulate the poor that, in our day, books are so cheap that a man may every year add a hundred volumes to his library for the price of what his tobacco and his beer would cost him. Among the earliest ambitions to be excited in clerks, workmen, journeymen, and, indeed, among all that are struggling up in life from nothing to something, is that of owning, and constantly adding to, a library of good books. A little library growing larger every year is an honorable part of a young man's history. It is a man's duty to have books. A library is not a luxury, but one of the necessaries of life."

Estimate.—This design was estimated to cost in stone, $4,000.

Paul Schulze del.

DESIGN. Nº 12.

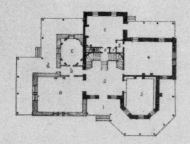 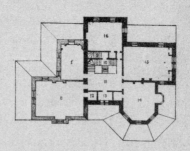

DESIGN No. 12.

FIRST FLOOR PLAN.

1. Veranda.
2. Hall, 20 × 22.
3. Library, 17 × 20.
4. Dining Room, 17 × 25.
5. Butler's Pantry.
6. Kitchen, 16 × 20.
7. Closet.
8. Passage.
9. Back Stairs.

SECOND FLOOR PLAN.

9. Back Stairs.
10. Main Stairs.
11. Hall.
12. Closet.
13. Bath Room.
14. Chamber, 17 × 20.
15. Do. 17 × 25.
16. Do. 15 × 20.

PROPOSED ADDITIONS.

a. Drawing Room, 17 × 25.
b. Passage.
c. Boudoir, 13 × 14.

d. Veranda.
e. Chamber, 17 × 25.
f. Do. 13 × 17.

HAVING shown in the preceding chapter how a small cottage or country seat, complete in itself, may contain as many elements of artistic beauty, and in every respect be quite as respectable as a more extensive mansion, we would now endeavor to explain how such a cottage may be built with reference to capacities for future enlargement and more ambitious proportions.

Though people sometimes make the apparent mistake of building too large for their present uses, much more frequently they commit the greater error of building without reference to any possible or probable increase of means and necessities. In time it often becomes essential to enlarge household accommodations, and then occur all those difficulties of alteration so often alluded to in this work, unless the dwelling was originally designed with reference to such probable alterations. Now, in order to prove that architecture can accommodate itself gracefully and easily to such changing conditions of life, provided the necessity for such accommodation is understood at the outset, we propose to arrange a plan which shall be such as to necessitate the immediate execution of only a part, but that part complete in itself, both inside and out.

By referring to the plan, it will be observed that, though extensive, only the dark portion is included in our perspective view, which comprises a house about equal, in capacity and accommodation, to the preceding design. The entrance hall, which is large enough to serve as a sitting room for the cottage, becomes a fitting appliance for the more stately extent of the future mansion.*

Now this is a complete cottage in itself, without the present necessity of any additions or alterations. But should the owner, at any future time, desire to enlarge, he can readily add the light portion of the plan, without interfering with the present structure. For a view of its external appearance, when enlarged, we refer the reader to Design No. 20, where it will be observed the additions blend and harmonize with the group, so that our simple country seat has grown naturally into nobler state, and assumed the air and dignity of a mansion. All of which shows the advantages of careful bringing up in young cottages.

There is no more frequent remark made by those who have built country houses, that "It has cost me much more than I intended expending." This tends to dissuade people from building, and they take refuge in the proverb: "Fools build houses and

* For further description of the interior, see Design No. 20.

wise men live in them." Why is it that so many shrewd business men are deceived in building? Why is it that a man having estimated an expenditure of $7,000, finds his completed residence to have cost $10,000, or even more? A satisfactory answer to this question may seem an arduous task, but we are confident it can be explained so as to be comprehended by all. When a man has an intention of building, he begins to "count the cost," and decides how much he will expend: he then sketches his idea of the general arrangement and the amount of accommodation necessary for his family, and he settles himself down to the belief that these ideas must be carried out at his original suppositions regarding the expense. In his calculation he relies, perhaps, on the "judgment" of a friend who has built, or on rude comparison with a neighbor's house, but undertakes to make no detailed estimate of the necessary number of feet of lumber, of the squares of roofing, yards of plastering, or the number of doors, windows, stairs, mantles, grates, or closets, none of the amount of stone and brick work, none of the painting, carting, grading, draining; he has thought nothing of the number of days' labor that will be necessary, of the price per day, of the outbuildings, wells, and cisterns, or of the task of preparing the grounds on which to build: of the actual expense of all these he has not the least idea, and the only wonder is that in his "rough guess" he has not been even more mistaken. With these mature ideas he goes to his builder as to an expert, to see what all will really cost, when, to his astonishment, he discovers that even a builder cannot supply him with the desired figures until complete plans and specifications have been prepared and thorough estimates made on them. He, perhaps, then leaves the builder in disgust, and has final recourse to the architect, who he finds unwilling to commit himself to any statement of amounts until drawings and estimates are made in a proper manner. The necessary papers are consequently ordered, and, when returned, he is surprised that the estimates exceed very considerably his proposed expenditure. When time and labor have thus been thrown away, he appeals, at last, to his architect to suit the plan to the price; and then he has a melancholy vision of the slow departure, under those unsparing hands, of many a little household comfort or luxury which he had permitted himself to cherish in his imagination, when laboring under his melancholy delusion of costs.

An intelligent understanding established in the outset between his means and his desires would have spared him much disappointment.

There is a simple rule which sometimes enables one to approximate the cost of the house he intends to build. It is to find a house of the general character and finish of that proposed; to calculate the number of cubic feet it contains from the basement floor to the top of the roof; to divide the cost of the building by the number of feet it contains, which, of course, gives the cost per foot. Reduce your proposed house to cubic feet, and multiply by the same price per foot. This will give you about the cost of your house, unless you should decide on a greater expense in finish. This rule, however, is a very uncertain one; it should be applied cautiously, and not too much confidence placed in its revelations.

Estimate.—This design would cost, in stone, about $5,500, and the additions about $3,500.

DESIGN Nº 13.

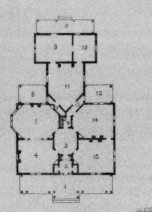

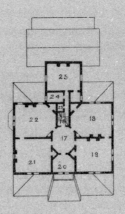

DESIGN No. 13.

THIS design represents another square building, containing all the advantages claimed for that form, yet so peculiarly arranged as to give, both within and without, a marked novelty and individuality of expression. The veranda-roof, over the front doorsteps, projects so as to break the great length of cornice, and might be made to combine utility with ornament, by allowing the steps to recede, which would afford ample shelter in alighting from carriages.

The tesselated vestibule is well lighted by stained glass sashes on either side the door. This vestibule contains two spacious closets for hats, coats, umbrellas, &c. The side opposite the entrance is spanned by an arch separating the outer from an inner vestibule, adorned with niches for statues on both sides. From this an ornamental ground-glass door gives access to a rotunda of large dimensions, occupying the centre of the house, and extending to the roof, where a stained glass skylight admits a pleasant, modulated light, more grateful in such an apartment than the white light of noon.

In this octagonal hall there are six doors symmetrically arranged, each of which opens into a separate room. Turning to the left, we enter by one of these doors a bay, occupying the centre of one side of a small parlor. Within this bay the door is balanced by a small statuary niche. The parlor opens into a large drawing room, through an arch supported by columns, affording a cheerful vista, closed by a fireplace which is studied so as to form one composition with two small flanking windows.

The form of the drawing room is octagonal, one side of which is occupied by a large bay window. In the four corners of this room are shown small niches for statues.

This room, like the small parlor, communicates directly with the rotunda, and by the two doors on the opposite side of the rotunda we may enter the library and dining room; the former of which has a similar arrangement in plan to the parlor, except that the chimney occupies the place of the arch. The dining room nearly corresponds in shape and disposition to the drawing room opposite, with the same exception in regard to the fireplace, and with the omission of the bay window. This room communicates with the kitchen through a rear entry, which also serves the purpose of a butler's pantry, and prevents the smells from the kitchen pervading the rest of the house. Another pantry will be observed, connected with the kitchen and corresponding with this entry. On the opposite side, the kitchen has a store or milk room, and a spacious laundry. In this arrangement there is no provision for back or private stairs; but the principal staircase is so shut off from the main body of the house, and communicates so directly with the apartments of the family and of the domestics, as to be equally accessible to both, without trespass on either hand.

Ascending the stairs, before we arrive at the top, we reach a landing affording access to a linen closet, bath and bedroom, the latter of which is provided with a commodious and well-lighted dressing room. Continuing the ascent, we come to the main portion of the second floor, and again enter the rotunda by a gallery (accidentally omitted in the drawing), which passes around it, communicating by doors with the five surrounding bedrooms. These bedrooms are amply supplied with closets and fireplaces, and are well lighted. This main stairway ascends to the attic, and is provided with a skylight. By the peculiar construction of the roof, good apartments are secured in the attic, for which light is obtained from gable and dormer windows. The facilities for ventilation in this design are worthy of remark, as through the well of the staircase, and especially through the rotunda, a constant circulation of air is produced throughout all the rooms. The main portion of the house may be heated from a register placed in the centre of the rotunda floor, under which stands the furnace.

From the number of niches shown throughout the house, we are induced to give a short extract from Wightwick's "Palace of Architecture," which may serve to show what appropriate parts

statuary and other works of art may be made to play in the duties
of hospitality and entertainment.

" The portico receives you with a readiness symbolized in the
statues of Invitation and Greeting, which occupy the niches on
each side of the door.

" In the two arched recesses, on either side the entrance-lobby,
are figures typifying Welcome and Hospitality; while the vestibule
is dignified by the presence of others, representing the Seasons, to
indicate that we keep open house the whole year, and shall, at all
times, be happy to see you.

" On the landing of the staircase are the statues of Fidelity and
Protection, to intimate that you may confide in our truth and
sleep in safety.

" The breakfast room is hung with a series of drawings by our
eminent water-color artist, bright, fresh, and crisp, as the morning
of Youth.

" From above the book cases, around our library, look down
the intelligent countenances of the literary great,—either beaming
with poetic thought, or grave with philosophic reflection,—and indicating the character of the works respectively ranged beneath
them.   The sculptured group at the end of the room represents a
boy rising from his completed studies, unconsciously to experience
those pure emotions of the heart, which form the Episode betwixt
youth and manhood.

" In one of the chambers of the tower is the only antique
treasure we possess, a sequel to the group last mentioned,—that
statue, unimprovable, which ' enchants the world,'—the *Venus de
Medicis.*

" The commingled pursuits of the drawing room are represented
by the poetry of History, the harmony of Landscape, the eloquence of gentle Portrait, and the charming varieties of Art repre-

senting Art, as in the architectural pictures of Claude and Cana-letti. The picture over the fireplace illustrates the beauty of Noon and the matured graces of Manhood.

" Upon the walls of the dining room glow the symbols of Fes-tivity, and the rich tints of the fruit-piece, with its crystal vessels, and the citron wreathing its golden coil around the goblet's silver stem. The principal picture represents Age, in its decline, enjoy-ing, with cheerful gratitude, the bread of its early industry.

" Connected with the dining room is the Conservatory, redolent with softest fragrance, and radiant with perfect beauty—an asylum for the gentler of Nature's offspring—yielding a corrective to the Sensual, who would deem purity insipid, and gently re-proving the Sanctimonious, who would regard external splendor as unholy. From indulging in the charms of nature's *loveliness*, you will next turn to the adoration of nature's GOD in our Chapel, where, over the altar, is seen the ' Man of Sorrows,' the ECCE HOMO of Guercino! The marble group of *Praise*, *Thanksgiving*, and *Prayer*, and the statue of *St. Paul*, are evidences of the skill and exalted feeling of the modern British Sculptor : and we shall here anticipate your surprise, at finding in our mansion only one specimen of the *Antique*, and so few works by the ' old masters.' Pardon us, then, for refusing to employ our private suite of apart-ments as a Museum of Miscellaneous Art. It has been our aim to make Painting and Sculpture coöperate with Architecture in the completion of a perfect whole, expressive of that character and of those affections which we desire to cultivate ; and as involving an uncompromising esteem for *fitness*, with an especial sympathy for *contemporary* good and beauty."

Estimate.—This design could be built for about $6,000.

Paul Schulze, del.

DESIGN, N.º 14.

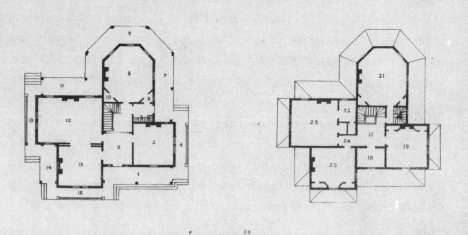

DESIGN No. 14.

OCCASIONALLY we find sites where the views in every direction are so pleasing that we desire to make them play their part in our household enjoyments, and be a continual blessing in our most frequented apartments. We would lose no feature of the landscape, and consequently must occupy our entire first floor with the family and reception rooms, while the kitchen and its offices must necessarily be placed below. The four sides of our house, then, must be taken up with parlor, dining room, drawing room, and library; and, in order that we may enjoy the views more openly and extensively, an ample disposition of veranda, balcony, and observatory seems especially appropriate.

At first sight it would appear that these considerations would be satisfied by the ordinary and vulgar arrangement of a square house, with a hall through the middle, a veranda all around, and an observatory on top. This is the pure and simple expression of what is called *sound judgment* in the matter, and as such it is entitled to respect. We only regret that this respect is accorded to such an extent that our country is filled with houses after this pattern, only varying in some minor point of detail, according to the whim of the builder. We propose, however, to prove that *good taste*, while according with sound judgment, meets the exigencies we have described more fully than this conventional pattern does, and obtains besides a work of beauty and grace. In short, we have here an emphatic repetition of the old and honorable architectural truth, that beauty and utility are never necessarily in discord one with the other. Let the reader judge for himself how far this is accomplished in the accompanying design.

It will be readily seen from the elevation, instead of proposing a square habitable box, we have indulged in some irregularity of outline and picturesqueness of feature, in our design. The practical advantage arising from this irregularity is, that each room commands a prospect in three distinct directions, without the aid of bays; all the windows open to the floor and give access to an outer platform, which, instead of being treated as a veranda, surrounding the house in the usual way, thereby darkening the rooms and disturbing the grand outlines, so that the house itself becomes secondary to its adjuncts, is managed as part balcony or terrace, protected by a bracketed canopy, and part veranda or porch, with the customary posts. This arrangement gives pleasing variety to the design, admits much more light into the principal apartments, and allows the outlines of the house to be prominently visible, from foundation to roof, at the corners.

The interior of this house is simple and convenient. The drawing room, which is of good size, connects with a less ambitious parlor by sliding doors. Directly opposite the drawing room is the library. This is in the most retired part of the house, adjoining no other room, and being central yet quiet. The dining room has an entrance from the main hall for family use, and also communicates with the private entry, where are the back stairs, which lead from basement to attic for the servants' accommodation. The form of this room is octagonal, one end being occupied by a three-sided bay, and the other made to correspond by cutting off the angles, thus producing a private passage, a pantry, and a china closet.

It may be asked where are the places for furniture, and more especially for a sideboard in this apartment? The window at the end opposite the entrance door is elevated above the rest, giving room for a sideboard to be placed under it, and is of an oval form composed of one sheet of plate glass like a mirror. The upper part of this sideboard should be made to form a frame for this window, so that the window will appear to be a part of the sideboard, and that a part of the room.

The peculiar arrangement of a window over the chimney-piece in the small parlor will be observed. This, though novel in our country, is quite common in Europe, and is often introduced with a happy effect. The mantlepiece, as usual, surmounts the fireplace, and the window frame above is gilt or otherwise treated like the frame of a looking glass, and is filled with a single sheet of plate glass. Such a contrivance produces an agreeable surprise, and enables persons sitting at the hearth to command a view of the scenery without, as if painted in a landscape by more than human art. But even this is attended by some objections unless guarded by another contrivance of equal ingenuity. It is objectionable when the sun is in such a quarter as to shine through it upon a person reading at the fire. This difficulty may be obviated by furnishing the window with a sliding shutter, which will answer the double purpose of security against burglars and a protection from an excess of light. Let the inside of this shutter be occupied by a landscape: then when closed it will have precisely the appearance of a finely framed picture hung over the mantlepiece. A mirror is sometimes used to play the same part. The flues of the chimney of course pass on either side the window, and operate quite as effectually as under the usual circumstances.

But let us turn from these pleasing fancies to the more practical subject of halls and bedrooms. The entrance hall, which is of good width, has placed in it, for the sake of economy, the main stairway, but it may be separated from the hall, if deemed desirable, by glass doors, thus obtaining a large, square, unoccupied vestibule. The chambers above are large and commodious; one having a dressing room, with two closets, where might be placed a bath room. Each of the other bedrooms is well supplied with closets, and the places for furniture are carefully studied.

A tower might be run up, with advantage, over the back stairs, but, anxious to show the reader how an observatory may be placed in the middle of the roof with good effect, the design has been arranged as shown.

Estimate.—This design, in wood, may be built for $6,000.

Paul Schutze, del.

DESIGN Nº 15.

Tint by H. Lawrence, 83. William St. N.Y.

DESIGN No. 15.

This design, which has an interior arrangement similar to that of No. 9, in the candor and simplicity with which it expresses the plan on which it is built, in the picturesque breaking of its sky-lines, with gables, hips, crests, and chimneys, its fair acknowledgment of all constructive obligations, and in its freedom from the cockney frippery of pretence, may serve as a fair illustration of the progress which American rural architecture has made since its days of Puritan plainness. But few specimens are now left of the real Puritan architecture of "the good old Colony times" in New England, or of the old stone revolutionary Dutch farm houses on the Hudson, or of the plantation houses of Maryland and Virginia, built by the first settlers with imported bricks. There is an old-world expression about these venerable buildings which recommend them to our interest as historical reminiscences. And it must be confessed that there is a truth and solidity about their construction which we look for in vain in the architecture of a later day. Undoubtedly they fairly express the solid energy, determination, and great-heartedness of the founders of a new empire in the wilderness. The straightforward respectability and honorable pride of the old Governors, are strongly imprinted upon their mansions. These are reproductions of the contemporary architecture of the mother country, England or Holland, so far as the limited

resources of a new country could reproduce it.　The prosperity of
the next generation, however, was too great and too rapid to preserve inviolate this marked self-respect and simplicity in architecture, and soon pretentious display, without the refinement of education, became the aim, finally settling into an era of domesticated
Greek temples and immense classic porticos in wood.　The true
refinement of the colonial aristocracy, the hearty hospitality of the
gentleman of the old school, seem to have been overwhelmed by
the pretentious show and glitter of a society whose " new-crowned
stamp of honor was scarce current," and which naturally in architecture developed a fever for base imitation, which it is one of the
special objects of this work to reprehend and criticise.　Apropos
to this, our readers will, perhaps, remember that in Coleridge's
narrative of the " Devil's Walk " it is related how

" He saw a cottage with a double coach-house,
　　A cottage of gentility;
And the devil did grin, for his darling sin
　　Is pride that apes humility."

The possession of wealth by the ignorant does not generally
bring with it an immediate, refining influence.　The plain, honest
man, who by integrity and enterprise has won for himself and
family a respectable name and an ample fortune, has, in the pursuit
of these ends, also acquired certain habits of thought and life more
honest and practical, than refined and elegant.　He leans rather
toward the useful than the beautiful, as is natural with those who
have had a hard struggle with the world.　In the latter part of
the last century and early part of the present, when our country
was yet young, were the *working days* of our people, and, so far as
regards art, therefore, it was truly *an iron age.*　The associations
of wealth, with less occupation of actual labor and more attention
to the amenities of life, necessarily lead to advanced ideas of edu-

cation and personal accomplishments, and thus the children are by one degree near to the refinement of the highest civilization. But early education and the force of early habits cannot be quite forgotten. Blood cannot be purified so soon. Yet a desire for knowledge, an ambition for improvement, has sprung up, and this stage of our part we may (to continue our figure) call the *silver age*. And so in the third age, the *golden*, we may expect to discover a higher tone, a more polished state of society; a culture observable, not only in manners and habits, but in the surroundings of life, in its elegancies no less than comforts, and in the nearer and more effectual union of the useful with the beautiful, the perfection of which is the acme of true refinement.

We may fairly suppose that our people are entering this new degree of civilization, and that their minds are beginning to cherish a national taste, made up of all the good points of the ruder eras of their history, combining the practical common sense and utility of the first with the ambition of the second, and the whole softened by the refinement of the third. Therefore, it is fitting for us to ascertain whether we are taking our proper position, nationally, in the world as lovers of art; whether we are assuming the insignia of progress; whether, for instance, government is founding national galleries of statuary and painting, collecting objects of art from the old world, and encouraging our own artists at home.

All this is not so foreign to our subject as may at first be thought. No one art can be entirely separated from the others, as the same æsthetic principles run through all. He who has cultivated a love for one branch of art, must have some sympathy for, and appreciation of, every other. No man can be a true lover of painting or sculpture, and not find pleasure in beholding the triumph of the sister art of architecture. Taking this as an index of popular artistic culture, we think we have reason to congratulate our readers on the happy prospects before us, as certainly of late years there has been evinced an increasing interest in architecture, both publicly and privately.   During the last ten years our advance has been rapid and certain, and full of promise.   Our public buildings at the National Capital compare favorably with similar buildings in other countries: our State Capitols, many of them, are well worthy of the important position they occupy; and generally our religious, municipal, and, indeed, all our public buildings, show that a great degree of interest in this subject has been aroused. And this interest bears its inevitable fruits.

With reference to rural architecture, the question may be asked, Why, especially in the vicinity of Boston, rural tastes seem more highly developed than in the suburbs of New York, or why in England are the people so universally chaste and elegant in this particular?   Is it not on account of the examples furnished in beautifying certain available portions of public grounds, in making parks and commons?   Does not this lead people to love rural culture and elegance, and induce them to enrich the appearance of their own homes in the surrounding country?

It has been observed, in reference to the Central Park of New York, that, when finished, wealthy persons will be content to live in town, finding there the pleasures which they have been in the habit of seeking in the country.   We think, on the contrary, the effect will be to educate a rural taste, and to create a passion where it never before existed, for an out-of-town life.   We believe that, from such impulses, in a few years the suburbs of New York will vie with those of any other city in the world.

The vignettes represent a rustic summer house and gateway, the former of which was built in New Jersey by A. Gerster.

Estimate.—This design, on account of its irregularity, would cost a trifle more than Design No. 9.

Paul Schulze, del.

DESIGN N⁰ 16.

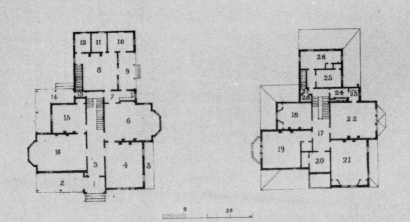

DESIGN No. 16.

THE accompanying villa, belonging to O. Benedict, Esq., is of an irregular Italian character, and was built in Bethel, one of those beautiful little towns in the interior of Connecticut, where manufacturing has become the chief interest of the inhabitants, and where industry and enterprise have received their proverbial reward.

At present there are but few trees on the place, and, therefore, verandas and canopies are resorted to for shade. The house is built of wood, the principal timbers being of pine, while the sills are made of chestnut. The frame is filled in with brick, and sheathed on the outside with rough hemlock boards, before the clapboards are put on. Generally one of these precautions is considered sufficient protection against the weather, but in exposed situations, where the wind has much power, the bricks serve to make the frame more solid, while the sheathing binds the building together, and effectually protects the house from inclemency of the weather. In using rough, external boarding, it is always well to have it placed diagonally, as it thus serves the purpose of bridging and strengthening the frame.

The interior of this house is arranged on a liberal scale. The main hall, which is spacious, contains the stairs, which are placed at the end to afford more room. The dining room has a niche for the sideboard, and communicates with the kitchen through a butler's pantry. This kitchen is provided with store, milk, and wash rooms. The ceilings of these are lower than those of the main house, making the rooms above, which are for servants, on a level with the landing of the main stairs. The rest of the chambers, provided on the second floor, are furnished with closets and places for furniture. Good bedrooms are constructed in the attic. Hot and cold water are carried throughout the house, which is heated by a furnace.

The owner has made provision for gas in all the rooms, this being supplied from private works upon his place; such works are now readily constructed at very moderate cost, and occupy but little room, while their arrangement is so simple and effective as to require but an hour's labor, of an ordinary workman, to obtain a fortnight's supply.

We would not ordinarily recommend the use of gas in a country house, unless a supply may be had from some public works; as too much machinery in a house of this kind, being liable to get out of order and need repairs, frequently causes great annoyance, in consequence of difficulties arising from the absence of mechanics. For the same reason we would not recommend the use of steam furnaces, extensive plumbing and similar works, unless it can be ascertained that the means for repairing are at hand. Gas, too, is not so indispensable an article as many of our countrymen might suppose. In the large cities of Europe it is excluded, in a great measure, from private houses, and in the palaces and dwellings of the nobility it is never introduced except for inferior purposes. During the visit of the Prince of Wales to this country it was the express stipulation of the Queen that no gas should be used in any of his apartments. At fashionable parties in our cities it is often superseded by wax candles.

The reasons for this prejudice are various. It is said, in the first place, to have an injurious effect upon the hair, eyes, and complexion; secondly, it is deemed plebeian in Paris, as there it is more or less associated with cafés and places of public amusement. A final and more potential reason is, that its intensity has not a favorable effect upon the delicate colors and shades of ladies' dresses, and we would say, confidentially, of course, that the injurious effect produced on the expression of their eyes, by the contraction of the pupil, may be avoided, without resort to belladonna, by shunning gaslight, and using some gentler means of obtaining artificial illuminations.

Estimate.—The estimates on this building were $7,000.

Paul Schulze del.

DESIGN N° 17.

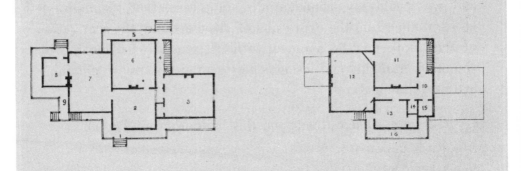

DESIGN No. 17.

THERE are several marked features about this design, which, we think, should recommend it to the attention of our readers. It possesses, in the first place, the advantage of a decidedly picturesque and irregular outline, without the usual complicated and expensive roofs which are generally considered essential to obtain the same result, and which, if not properly constructed, are liable to need frequent repairs, and to form lodging places for snow and ice—a very material objection, considering the length and severity of our northern winters. It is not meant by this that irregular roofs are necessarily subject to such inconveniences, but simply that roofs of this description have not generally sufficient attention given them in design to avoid these dangers. Irregular roofs are often taken from foreign examples, which are not exposed to the same contingencies of weather, and so not unfrequently indulge in valleys and reëntering angles, which, reproduced in our climate, are fatal to the tightness of the roof. Yet, if properly managed, irregular roofs may act better to shed the heavy falls of snow, than many of the more flat examples, which are perfectly plain and regular.

Another feature in this design is a saving of the expense of verandas by the adoption of balconies and terraces in their stead. These extend around the principal rooms both on the first and second stories, those in the latter position serving as a protection for the terraces below, and are themselves sheltered by the projection of the main roof of the building. The expense of a finished underpinning is also avoided by heaping the earth around the house, in the manner of a terrace, up to the first-story beams, leaving openings for window views, and keeping the cellar warm and dry. By this contrivance the house has what most buildings seem to lack, a base or firm footing upon the ground. It seems to afford a closer connection between the earth and the building, giving the architecture more the appearance of growing out of nature and being its offspring, than of being the handiwork of man, and placed by him formally upon its lap.

This house may be used as a *cottage orné*. The entrance is approached by steps, forming a part of the terrace. We enter at once the main hall, which, unobstructed by stairs, may be occupied as a spacious sitting room. The dining room is entered on the right of this hall, through an arched alcove. The position of the windows, doors, and fireplace in this room, is carefully studied to give symmetry. Access is obtained directly from the dining room into the staircase hall, which may be approached with equal facility from the rear of the building and from the entrance hall. The stairway thus treated has its several advantages: from its privacy it obviates the necessity of a servants' staircase, and is in direct communication with the basement, kitchen, dining room, outside entrance, second story, and attic. The library is a large room with broad, unbroken walls on either side for books, a fireplace in front and one large window in the rear, thus preventing cross light and giving the occupant, when seated before the fire, the light upon his book rather than in his eyes. The drawing room, which is on the left, has a small cabinet attached. The chamber-floor is divided into commodious rooms provided with closets, a bath room, and linen closet.

But this design, with some slight alterations, would more appropriately serve the purpose of a *double lodge*, accompanying a mansion, the first floor being occupied by the farmer, or, perhaps, the lodge keeper, and the second by the gardener, who would approach his apartments by the balcony staircase. Should the gardener reside elsewhere on the place, this second story might be fitted up as a billiard room, the floor being well deafened to prevent disturbing the family below.

These internal arrangements are susceptible of easy alteration to suit such fancies, and any clever architect can readily adapt the building to serve any of these purposes.

Estimate.—This house, if plainly built, would cost about $3,500.

Paul Schulze. del.

DESIGN N⁰ 18.

DESIGN No. 18.

It is usual with persons about purchasing a country residence, to desire to find a place where "improvements," as they are called, have already been made, where the outbuildings have been erected, and the trees have attained a considerable size. The house may not be exactly equal to their requirements, and it is vainly imagined that by adding a wing here and a bay window there, with some alteration of doors, the patching of a few leaks, and the aid of new paint and paper, it may be made to answer all the purposes required. The alterations are hardly begun before the owner finds that, instead of a few patches in the roof, it is so far gone as to demand an entirely new one. In remodelling the rooms, the old work does not at all correspond with the new, and some of it is so far decayed as to be actually unworthy the house. The style of the house, too, is out of keeping, and so many and constant are the suggested alterations, that an entire renovation is needed. After repeated attempts to make the old work match the new, the building is, with protracted difficulties, completed, though in a most unsatisfactory manner. The house, even as renovated, contains so many disadvantages that we are reminded of the proverbial impropriety of putting new wine in old bottles; and when it is too late, the owner begins the old story of wishing he had followed the advice of his architect and abandoned at the outset the idea of altering, since, with the same expense, he might have had an entirely new house, and one completely satisfactory. In the grounds, too, perhaps, from which he had anticipated so much pleasure, he often finds himself disappointed, as, after some experience, he discovers that they in no part accord with modern taste in landscape gardening. The land has been cleared of its natural growth of oak and chestnut, which so nobly adorned it, to make room for formal rows of fruit trees.

The vignette at the left will serve as an example of the abortions we so often find disfiguring the most beautiful sites throughout our land. It was built as a public boarding house, and is situated on one of those charming points, so much admired, on the north side of Long Island Sound, just east of the village of Stamford, Conn., and notwithstanding its unattractive appearance, its delightful location made it a favorite summer resort for families from town.

It has recently been purchased by John Howland, Esq., of New York. It was a matter of some doubt, in the mind of this gentleman, what disposition to make of the building, as it was too large for a farm house and inferior as a dwelling. It was finally determined to attempt to convert it into a respectable country seat, and the accompanying design was prepared for that purpose, with what success the reader must decide for himself.

The ceilings were much too low. This difficulty we were enabled to overcome, on the first story, by proposing to raise the house bodily above the foundations, leaving the floor in its present position and filling up below. The attic beams were raised to give greater height to the second story. The rooms were too small, and the main stairs obstructed the hall, but by altering some partitions the rooms were readily enlarged, and the stairs were removed to an alcove in the hall. The design, on completion, was submitted to the owner, who, though he confessed himself satisfied at the result, rather than alter at so great an expense, wisely concluded to convert the structure into a farm house, with few alterations, and to build a new residence on a choice site, which should, in every particular, accord with his own ideas and wants.

The vignette at the right represents a summer house and ice house combined. It was designed for Mr. Howland, in accordance with the following suggestions of Mr. B. S. Carpenter, in "The Rural New Yorker:"

"The perfect success which I met in keeping ice last summer, I think, is owing largely to a new principle involved in the building; therefore I speak of the plan for the consideration of those who are about to build for that purpose. Instead of one hollow wall for a non-conductor of heat, as in ordinary ice houses, I have two, with a space between them for confined air. The site is on a gravel slope. The foundation, for convenience in storing ice, is dug two feet below the surface of the ground. The outside wall for non-conducting material is six inches in the clear. The inside walls are four inches, with space for confined air of four inches. The doors for entrance correspond perfectly with the hollow walls in thickness, and are filled in the same manner—being shaped to shut with a bevel edge, like the doors to safes used by merchants and bankers. At the lower side of the plates is a ceiling, upon which I put spent tan one foot thick, which tan is in direct connection with the side walls, so that any settling in the walls may be supplied from overhead. From the under side of the ceiling runs a ventilator, with a hole of one and a half inch bore, up through the roof, and is finished with an ornamental cap.

"The room for ice is eight by ten feet in the clear, and eight feet high. Without a more minute description, I think the building will be understood. If not, inquire further, any who wish to do so. About all the waste of ice that I observed during the summer was at the bottom; and this was so slow that we used the ice without regard to economy, for a large family, and in a dairy of thirty-five cows, besides giving freely to our neighbors.

"I put sticks four inches thick at the bottom to put ice on, and also some straw about the sides as well as underneath the ice."

Paul Schutze del.

DESIGN № 19.

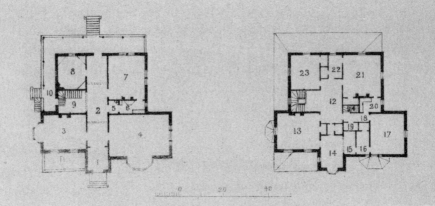

0   20   40

DESIGN No. 19.

THIS suburban villa was designed for Mrs. T. D. Wheeler, and executed in Prospect street, New Haven. It is pleasantly situated opposite the beautiful grounds belonging to the Hillhouse family. The exterior bears an English character, bordering somewhat upon the Tudor, but slightly Americanized by the addition of verandas. Perhaps the English Tudor or late Gothic cottage is more readily adapted to our houses here in America than almost any other, as it had its growth in very nearly the same domestic exigencies which hold good with us, and its great *pliability* of style renders it applicable to dwellings of almost any extent or peculiarity of plan. The readiness with which its steep roofs shed the frequent rains and snows of our climate is another cogent reason for its more gen. eral adoption.

This house is built of brick, with hollow walls, stuccoed on the outside, and colored a neutral tint. This mode is somewhat confined to this locality, where it is practised with considerable success. The roof is covered with slate, from the Vermont quarries, with the exception of a small flat or deck on top, which is covered with tin, and used for the purpose of collecting water for the tank in the attic. By reference to the first floor plan, the reader will perceive that the accommodations are of a liberal character. The main hall is entered through a spacious vestibule; this is paved with encaustic tile, and well lighted by a window at the side. Folding doors of plate glass give entrance into the hall. This hall is nine feet wide by thirty-eight feet in length, and entirely unobstructed, the stairs being placed at the side. Halls of this kind are usually objectionable, from presenting a long and naked appearance, and being dark in the centre. These objections are, however, here, in a great measure, remedied; the monotonous extent of the hall being broken by two arches, as indicated by dotted lines, and additional light being obtained from the stairway at the side. There is another exit from this hall without going to the extreme end, which is at the left, under the main stairs, where sufficient headway is obtained to admit a good-sized door. This, then, renders that portion of the main hall beyond the staircase superfluous, if great economy of room is desirable, and it might be included in the study, making this room equal in size to the library. The present arrangement is, however, considered far preferable for considerations of free ventilation, for a promenade in bad weather, and for the generous effects of ample space obtained on entering the house.

The two principal rooms, viz., drawing room and library, are large, and provided with spacious bay windows. The doors entering these rooms are opposite each other, and might be made double, thus, as occasion required, throwing the suite into one grand apartment, including the hall. The dining room is of good size, and is connected with a large butler's pantry, which is provided with a sink, dresser, and dumb waiter, communicating with a similar pantry below, opening into the kitchen. A very convenient addition to a dwelling of this kind is a gentleman's wash closet on the first floor; such an one is provided here, connecting with the main hall, and also serving as a passage to the butler's pantry. The grand feature of this house, next to the hall, is, undoubtedly, the stairway, which occupies a large space at the left, and is well lighted by a stained glass window. Too often, in allowing the stairs to ascend through the hall, both features are spoiled, the hall being cut up and its continuity destroyed, and the stairs themselves made tiresome by their long, straight, unbroken rise to the floor above, no landing intervening as a happy resting place in the ascent.

The study is, perhaps, the most agreeable and attractive feature of the house. Its chimney, it will be observed, is placed diagonally in one corner of the room, while the other three are filled with corresponding diagonal book cases. The mantel is of richly carved black walnut, and the book cases, wainscoting, ceiling, and doors of the room are also elaborately designed and executed in hard wood, the whole oiled and polished. The brick flue from the fireplace recedes above the opening, giving space for a cabinet over the mantel, which well balances the book cases. These all extend to the ceiling, and their heavy oaken cornices and bases skirt the entire room. The furniture of the room is appropriately of carved oak. The owner has recently enclosed with glass a portion of the south veranda, opposite the study windows, for a greenhouse on a moderate scale.

The chambers are all commodiously arranged; two of them communicating with the bath room, and having separate dressing rooms. All the rooms have closets, while linen and cedar closets are separately provided.

The plumbing is economically arranged, as, the tank, bath room, butler's pantry, and kitchen being directly over each other, long lines of horizontal piping are avoided. These are, however, unfortunately, on the north side of the house, where they might be affected by frosts; but this is guarded against by their being packed in sawdust and coming in contact with the kitchen chimney. The drains are purposely made small, as by this means the liquids run through with greater rapidity, and act effectually to keep the drain pipes free from obstructions.

Estimate.—The estimates on this house were $13,000.

Paul Schulze, del.

DESIGN N°. 20.

DESIGN No. 20.

THIS design, which is an enlargement of No. 12, and whose plan is shown on that plate, we shall now attempt to describe in detail.

The entrance hall, as before stated, is large, and well worthy the extent of the mansion. Its floor is composed of narrow, hard wood boards, with a border of a different color, and a mosaic centre around the register. The walls are wainscoted with black walnut, and the doors and trimmings are of the same. The staircase, which is the principal feature, is also composed wholly of this material, and occupies the entire rear of the hall; it ascends, as we noticed, in two flights from the right and left to the landing, and continues thence in a single flight to the floor above. The ceiling of this staircase is supported by carved wood ribs, which continue across the hall and intersect with the mouldings of the front door; these ribs are repeated elsewhere across the ceiling, forming panels, which are ceiled with narrow oak boards, unless, for economy, plaster should be preferred, in which case a delicate sky-blue tint might be used with good effect. The library, which is finished in the same appropriately grave but rich manner, has walnut book cases extending to the ceiling, the cornices of which run around the room. This apartment communicates with the hall by folding doors, and, the drawing room opposite having a similar communication, the whole range of apartments may be thrown into one suite when occasion requires. The drawing room is of large dimensions, but, instead of being finished in natural wood, has its floor carpeted for the sake of the warmth, comfort, and color so essential in an apartment which is the social centre and abiding place of the household. Its ceiling and walls are painted with brilliant tones of vermilion, cobalt, and gold, on a ground of some delicate tint. The mantel is of Italian marble, while those in the library and dining room are of carved walnut and oak. The latter room, though receiving a similar finish to the hall, should be of oak instead of walnut. In all these rooms the furniture must of course correspond with their respective styles of architectural treatment, the furniture of the dining room being of carved oak, and that of the hall and library of walnut. These woods should in no case be varnished, but oiled and polished, while the hard wood floors should be waxed. Carpets for these floors would be entirely out of place, but mats and rugs may be used with elegant effect. In the drawing room, rosewood furniture, with the richest carpets and gilded mirrors, are highly appropriate. The hall has a side external entrance, at the entry B, which connects with the boudoir and drawing room. The boudoir has a fireplace located diagonally in one corner, the flue of which opens into the kitchen chimney. The other corners are similarly occupied by cabinets. This is the private room of the mistress of the house, and is in direct communication with both the family and domestic portions of the establishment. By a slight alteration of the private stairway, a door might be arranged connecting this room with the kitchen, through a closet.

The kitchen, which is large, connects with the dining room through a butler's pantry, and is also conveniently placed with reference to the hall, which, when desired, is large enough to be used as a breakfast or tea room. The second story contains five chambers, a bath room, and linen closet, and in the attic are good bedrooms.

The vignette at the left illustrates a bit of rock work with a rustic bridge over a brook, as executed at Central Park by A. Gerster, showing how picturesque the simplest natural feature may be made. That on the right represents a boat and bathing house, placed some distance from the shore, to secure deep water, and approached by a bridge. The whole is ornamentally designed, but sufficiently strong to withstand any storm.

Paul Schulze del.

DESIGN N⁰ 21.

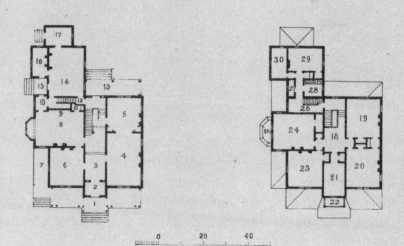

0   20   40

DESIGN No. 21.

THIS building was erected at Danbury, Conn., for A. E. Twee dy, Esq. The material of which it is constructed is unbaked brick, made of concrete, and is somewhat similar to, though much more durable than, that of the ordinary gravel or rough-cast walls, which have so often been attempted, and nearly as often proved failures.

In the interior of the country, where stone may not be readily obtained, and brick and lumber can be transported only at great expense, this material will be found of great advantage, as it can be manufactured on the spot, from the loose gravel that comes from the excavation of the cellar, provided the gravel is sharp, and free from loam or clay. The material is then mixed in the proper proportion with lime or cement, placed in moulds, and subjected to great pressure. The bricks thus formed are carefully placed on boards, where they remain until the mortar is set. They are then perfectly hard and ready for use. The size of these bricks is ten inches long, by five inches wide and four inches deep, with a hollow space in the centre, which prevents dampness passing through. This latter object is also aided by the manner in which the walls are laid, the joints being "*broken*," as it is called. The hollow space in the outside brick just covering the solid portion of the brick behind, it is impossible for dampness to penetrate.

The manner in which these bricks are made renders them perfectly smooth and square. They are of a neutral gray tint, which could not be improved as a color for the house. They require no paint, but only an occasional coat of boiled oil, for the purpose of better resisting the weather.

It is particularly necessary, however, that persons building with this material should employ the most experienced workmen for making it, since, if the proportions and method of manufacture are not exactly understood, this brick is apt to be weak and porous, and consequently to prove unsafe; but if proper precautions are taken, actual experience has proved that it is among the cheapest and best materials for building. Mr. Tweedy's house has the interior plaster laid directly upon the brick, so that the important items of lathing and furring are avoided in the bill of expenses, and he assures the author that he has never discovered any dampness upon the inside walls. The woodwork of the house is nailed directly on the brick, so that there is no occasion for introducing the usual wooden blocks, which are liable to shrink and decay, and thereby weaken the walls. The following letter from Mr. Tweedy may prove interesting, as it gives his opinion in this mat. ter, and somewhat of the history of his house :

"DANBURY, *May* 2, 1859.

" HENRY HUDSON HOLLY, ESQ. :

" DEAR SIR : I have neglected till now writing you in answer to yours of 18th April, in relation to what is called the Foster brick, from which my house is built. I have the fullest confidence in them, if they are made of the right material, and properly manufac- tured. Ten parts of clean grit or coarse sand to one part of lime is the mixture used for the blocks for the outside course of my house. About five per cent. of cement was added to the above mixture. My house is about 40 feet square, main body, two sto- ries and attic ; walls 28 feet in height, 10 inches in thickness. The L or kitchen part, two stories, about 20 by 24 feet. I began building two years since, laid the walls 21 feet high, to attic floor timbers ; stopped the latter part of October; covered. the tops of the walls with boards, and left the building open and exposed during the Winter and Spring of 1857 and 1858, and found the walls all sound and solid. In May last, carried up the walls, and completed the outside and partition walls during last Summer and Fall ; and now the building is as strong and solid as any brick can be. Although my house may be considered an experiment here, for one of the size—three or four smaller ones having been built of the same material in the mean time—I should have the fullest confidence in putting up a building of any size, with the experience now had in making the bricks.

" My inside plastering is put on without furring and lathing, on the outside walls, and is perfectly dry and solid. It is my opinion, with suitable arrangements for making the blocks, the saving over ordinary clay burnt bricks will be 25 or 30 per cent. per cubic foot in the walls. Any information in regard to the material and building will be cheerfully given by

" Yours, respectfully,

(Signed.)　　" A. E. TWEEDY."

Estimate.—The estimates on this house were $12,500.

Paul Schulze, del.

DESIGN Nº 22.

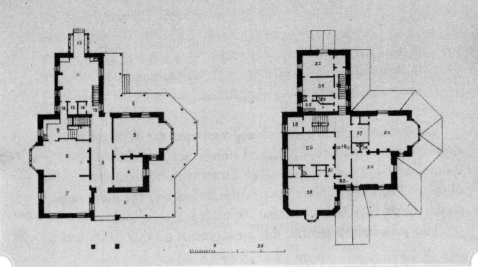

DESIGN No. 22.

THIS building was designed and executed for William R. Fosdicke, Esq., of Stamford, Conn., and stands on the summit of a rising ground north of the village, called Strawberry Hill, from which is obtained one of the finest views of the Sound and the surrounding country that may be had in that vicinity.

The principal object in the arrangement of this house was to bring all the rooms into such a position that each might have the advantage of the view which is on the veranda side, toward the south. The disposition of apartments on the ground floor, accordingly, is such that but one of them is without this advantage. This happens to be the dining room, which is seldom occupied for any other than its legitimate purpose; therefore, exterior views are of comparatively small consideration. This room might have been made to exchange places with the kitchen, and thereby have received the same advantage; but this would have brought the latter into too close proximity with the family apartments, and the dining room would not have been so pleasantly situated. The owner was also anxious to have it connect with the drawing room, by sliding doors. For these reasons the plan resolves itself into the present arrangement. These sliding doors, it will be remarked, are placed on the broad side of the room instead of at the end, which is the usual mode. By this plan the doors may be made much wider, and the two broad sides of each room being thus joined give more the appearance of a single large apartment.

The symmetrical arrangement of these rooms adds very much to their beauty. Exactly opposite the fireplaces in each are windows; the bay window in the dining room is crowned with a Gothic arch, corresponding to similar ones over the sideboard niche and sliding doors. The windows and doorheads throughout this floor terminate in a similar manner, and the whole house, both outside and in, has a decidedly Gothic sentiment, partaking principally of the characteristics of the Tudor period.

The grand external feature of this house is the veranda, which extends across the entire southern portion. This, though running along the side of the kitchen, has no connection with it, as the servants are provided with a spacious porch at their entrance door. The laundry and milk room are placed in the basement, under the kitchen, which communicates with an area under the veranda, making them, in fact, rooms above ground.

The furnace is placed in the centre of the cellar, and under the main hall. This cellar is provided with a coal slide and several bins, convenient to the furnace, for the different kinds of coal. The milk-room door is constructed with panels, which may be opened to obtain a draft from the opposite window—an essential requisite in a room of this kind.

The cellar walls are built of twenty-inch stonework, the bottom being composed of large flags projecting six inches on either side, and laid in concrete. This footing course serves a double purpose: as a base for the stonework, preventing the building from settling, and also as a safeguard from rats. It is the nature of this animal, in getting into a house, to burrow down by the side of the foundation walls, but, when coming in contact with a stone or other impediment, to return and start anew rather than go around the obstacle. This six-inch projection acts, therefore, as a formidable barrier against the entrance of vermin. The several floors, also, are deafened, thus not only preventing the communication of sound, but leaves no space between ceiling and floor for rats to occupy.

In a building of this kind, outside blinds are not only out of place, but impracticable, as the moulded lables or drips above the windows would prevent them from swinging around. Inside sliding or folding blinds must therefore be substituted. These are much more convenient, as they may be opened or closed without raising the windows, which in cold and stormy weather is objectionable, and in a house with thick walls there is always sufficient room in the window jambs for a box to receive these blinds. The windows opening on the veranda are peculiar, being a combination of French and sliding sash. The difficulty of these has generally been that they cannot be made sufficiently tight to exclude the rain and cold of our northern winters, while the latter cannot be easily made to slide up high enough to give proper headway for passing in and out. These combine the two advantages of security and providing ample headway, the first by sliding, the second by swinging, in the ordinary manner, when raised above the weather sill. Another advantage possessed by these over common swinging sashes, is that they may be opened, to admit air, without interfering with curtains or inside blinds.

Estimate.—The estimates on this house were $10,000.

Paul Schulze del.

DESIGN Nº 23.

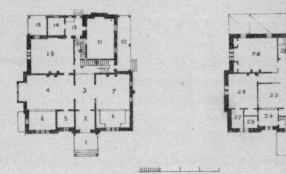

DESIGN No. 23.

THE irregularity and diversity of outline in this building are intended to accord with a picturesque locality, or, by the variety of its skylines, as seen above surrounding trees, to offer a pleasing indication from afar of domestic comfort and hospitality, and of an extensive household. The plan, with the exception of the projection of the kitchen, approaches a square, thus obtaining economy in walls, although the general effect of the structure affords the impression of an irregular plan.

The entrance, which should always be the most prominent external object, is here placed in the tower itself, and rendered still more conspicuous by the large, hospitable porch, which seems to extend a welcome even before we enter. This porch furnishes a sort of footing for the tower, and the veranda and buttress serve as a base for the house itself, and overcome the abruptness of formal walls springing directly from the ground. The interior of the building is arranged for comfort, combining utility with ornamental design. The vestibule is large, and might have a closet for coats taken off the cabinet on the left. It is separated from the main hall by folding doors of plate glass. The first thing that attracts the eye, on entering this hall, is the beginning of the stairs, starting up into a sort of L, which conceals the most of the staircase from view, exhibiting only the newel and a small part of the rail; these, if properly treated, may be made highly ornamental, giving to the entire hall a marked character and expression. These stairs are somewhat cut off from the main hall by an arch, represented on the plan by dotted lines. Between this arch and vestibule are broad sliding doors opening into the drawing room on one side and the library on the other, thus obtaining a fine vista through the house.

The drawing room has opening from it a small cabinet, which is often a very pretty addition. It may be used as a private office or small reception room, and have a door opening into the vestibule. At the left of this is a large music alcove or bay, separated from the drawing room simply by an arch. The library has a similar alcove, used for books, thus leaving the main portion unobstructed for a sitting room. By the introduction of curtains, this alcove might be converted into a place for reading. The dining room is symmetrical, and has a niche for a sideboard opposite the fireplace. Its connection with the kitchen is through a spacious entry, also used as a butler's pantry, and containing a sink, dresser, &c. This entry also communicates with a back staircase and store room, and has an external entrance for servants. The rear entrance for the family is at the end of the main hall, under the staircase, where sufficient headway is obtained for a full-sized door.

The second floor is provided with a bath and five spacious bed rooms, all with studied places for furniture and large closets. Two have dressing rooms, and a third is provided with an alcove similar to that in the drawing room, from which we may enter, on one side, the bath, on the other, a dressing room. Both staircases extend to the attic, where are servants' rooms, spare chambers, and billiard room. Here, too, the observatory stairs begin. The front of this house commands but a limited view, for which reason the best rooms and verandas are placed in other parts of the building.

Estimate.—This building, in stone, would cost about $12,000.

Paul Schulze del.

DESIGN № 24.

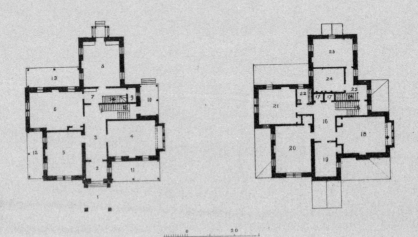

DESIGN No. 24.

THIS house is designed with particular reference to durability and facilities for warming and ventilating. No perishable material is used in its construction. The walls are built of stone; the partitions, where the proper support is obtained, are of brick, and elsewhere of galvanized lath; the window frames are of iron, and all the floors of cement, with a strip at the side for securing carpets. The roof is of slate, while the stairs and inside trimmings are entirely of metal or composition. Thus the building is rendered secure from the ravages of fire and from decay.

Much has already been said on the importance of ventilation, yet there is danger of doing too much as well as too little in this matter. The subject has become almost a monomania with some, and it is imagined that, unless there are top and bottom injecting and ejecting flues, arranged on scientific principles, and so complicated as to keep both mind and body continually in action in the management of them, the air must be poisonous.

Again, we see the same wild schemes in regard to heating. The idea prevails, to a certain extent, that a hot-air furnace is, of all things, most injurious; that the heat generated by it consumes instantly and effectually the vital properties of the atmosphere. Therefore, hot-air furnaces are condemned *in toto*, and steam, hot water, and other complicated and expensive contrivances are resorted to.

The fact is, that the fault is often more in the owner than in the furnace. A man purchasing a furnace for the purpose of heating his house frequently contents himself with one of the smallest possible size to save expense, knowing that, although the amount of air passing through it will be small, yet, by heating that small amount red hot, it will warm his house. Undoubtedly this object will be effected, but no less surely will the oxygen of the air be burnt out with such violent heat, and the lungs, habitually inhaling this parched and vitiated atmosphere, be much injured thereby. Were he to expend a trifle more for a furnace which would introduce a larger volume of air, moderately heated, he would find that air as soft and pleasant as that radiated from steam or hot water, and at the same time he would procure a saving in fuel, and perhaps still more in doctors' bills.

The only advantage we perceive in the steam and water furnaces over those constructed for hot air, is the impossibility of producing by their agency more than a certain degree of heat. Therefore, in order to have a sufficient amount, the radiating surface must be increased in proportion to the extent of space to be warmed; while the superiority of the hot-air furnace must be evident from its greater simplicity of construction and its costing but about one third.

" Modern improvements " are excellent things until used in excess, and they then become more troublesome than useful. This is especially true of ventilation; for, however complicated an arrangement may be requisite in a public building for this purpose, yet, in a dwelling, the more simple the method, the more effectually it will act. It is perhaps difficult to say which, among so many, is the best system, but we would suggest the following as simple and effective.

We will suppose our house to be heated with, say, one of Boynton's hot-air furnaces of large dimensions, so that the fresh air flows from it throughout the building in no way diminished in purity, but merely changed by having the chill taken off and rendered mild and delightful. Warm air, as we are all aware, has a tendency to rise; hence, if we place our ventilator at the ceiling, the flow of air will be in a direct line from the register to it, and thus only that portion of the room which lies between these points will be either warmed or ventilated. Where, then, shall the opening for ventilation be? Placing it at the bottom of the room, the warm air rises, as before, to the ceiling, but, finding no escape there, it must seek a downward channel; and if now the opening be on the opposite side from the register, all the air in the room must be kept in motion. We thus obtain an atmosphere pure, and, at all seasons, as agreeable as that of summer. It remains to describe the construction of the ventilating flue. Every room in our house, of course, has a fireplace, though we have obviated, in a great measure, the necessity of fires. Here is unquestionably the place for the ventilator, and the whole complicated mystery of successful heating and good ventilation is solved by a large hot-air furnace in the cellar and a fireplace in every room. We would also advise, as a material assistance in the work of ventilation, a little fire in the grate, securing, by this, a better draught, and requiring less heat in the furnace. The old style of anthracite grates has almost fallen into disuse, and the English soft-coal grates are taking their place. Soft coal is not only more cheerful, reminding us of the good old days of wood fires, but its effect is not so drying upon the air.

If wood or bituminous coal is used, however, the chimney flues should be built larger, as they otherwise are apt to become obstructed by soot. Finally, we would recommend the use of double sashes in winter, by which a great deal of cold air is excluded.

Estimate.—This building, in stone, would cost about $11,500.

Paul Schulze del.

DESIGN N.º 25.

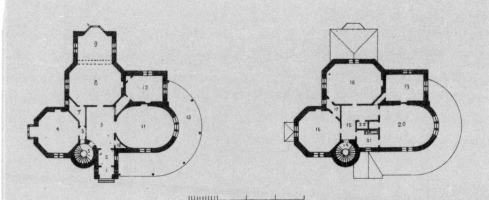

DESIGN No. 25.

A BUILDING like this, which is of the feudal or castellated style, should be adopted only with the greatest caution, as the contrast between modern and feudal life is so great that, without a nice adaptation of circumstances, it may appear ridiculous to build, and much more ridiculous to occupy, such an establishment. This style, referred to in Chap. I., is similar to that which existed prior to the union of the Houses of York and Lancaster, after which event there no longer existed any necessity for private fortifications.

The following extract from an English writer will give the reader some idea of an edifice of this kind:

"The situation of castles of the Anglo-Norman kings and barons was most commonly on an eminence and near a river—a situation eligible on several accounts. The whole site of the castle (which was frequently of great extent and irregular figure) was surrounded by a deep and broad ditch, sometimes filled with water, and sometimes dry. Before the great gate was an outwork called a barbican, which was a strong and high wall, with turrets upon it, for the defence of the gate and drawbridge. On the inside of the ditch stood the wall of the castle, about ten feet thick and twenty feet high, with battlements on top; on this wall, at proper distances, high, square towers were built, which served for lodging some of the principal officers, and on the outside were erected, lodgings for the common servants or retainers, granaries, store houses, and other necessary offices, and on the flat roofs of these buildings stood the defenders of the castle, when it was besieged, and from thence discharged arrows, darts, and stones on the besiegers. The great gate of the castle stood in the course of this wall, and was strongly fortified with a tower on each side, and rooms over the passage, which was closed with folding doors of oak, often plated with iron, and with an iron portcullis, or gate, let down from above. Within this outward wall was an open space, or court, in which stood frequently a church or chapel. Here, also, was another ditch, wall, gate, and tower, enclosing the inner court, within which the chief tower, or keep, was built, which was the residence of the baron. Underground were dismal, dark vaults, for the confinement of prisoners, called the dungeon. In this building, also, was the great hall, in which the owner displayed his hospitality, by entertaining his numerous friends and followers. At one end of the great hall was a place raised a little above the rest of the floor, called the *dais*, where the chief table stood, at which persons of the highest rank dined. Though there were unquestionably great variations in the structure of castles and palaces in this period, yet the most perfect and magnificent of them seem to have been constructed on the above plan. Such, to give an example, was the famous castle at Bedford, as appears from the following account of the manner in which it was taken by Henry III., A. D. 1224: 'The castle was taken by four assaults. In the first was taken the barbican; in the second the outer ballia, or court; at the third attack, the wall by the old tower was thrown down by the miners, when, with great danger, they possessed themselves of the inner ballia, through a chink; at the fourth assault, the miners set fire to the tower, so that the smoke burst out, and the tower itself was cloven to that degree, as to show visibly some broad chinks, whereupon the enemy surrendered.' "

After the age of Edward I., we find another kind of castle introduced, approaching nearer to the idea of modern palaces. The first was that of Windsor, built by Edward III. This convenient and enlarged style of building was soon imitated on a lesser scale by the nobles of the realm, and two remarkable instances, wherein convenience and magnificence were singularly blended at this period, may be found in the castles of Harewood and Spofford, in Yorkshire. The improvements at Kenilworth afford another instance of the great enlargement which the English castles received during this age. Of course, a full description of these feudal residences need not be entered into here, especially as this has already been done by other and abler writers. For descriptions of this kind, the reader is referred to the works of Sir Walter Scott, and more particularly Kenilworth and Ivanhoe.

Shortly after this period gunpowder was invented, which, instead of bringing war and bloodshed into the world, proved the most effectual means of preventing them. The people of England, instead of requiring castellated residences, now put their trust in their " wooden walls," and their fighting was done far away from their native shores. Their private strongholds were soon in ruins, dismantled by shot and shell; and with the dissolution of feudalism, the mind of the nation soon broke the cords which had bound it for so many centuries; a ray of light dawned, and the " dark ages " dated among the things that were. From this time until Tudor architecture was fully established in England, a style between the castellated and that described in No. 27 was generally adopted for domestic dwellings, of which the accompanying design is an attempted imitation. It will be observed that all the old contrivances to obtain strength and seclusion are here omitted, and comfort and convenience are substituted. The walls, for example, are no thicker than ordinary walls, and the windows, instead of being mere warlike loopholes, are of ample, peaceful dimensions, and are filled with glass. Here, too, we have committed the anachronism of introducing chimneys and bay windows, with, what is still more unusual in castles, a porch without a portcullis, and a veranda. All these, however foreign to the requirements of a castle, are yet of use to us, and whatever style we may adopt, we do not hesitate to add to it, to the best of our ability, any improvement which convenience or necessity may require. Yet all such additions must be treated with the greatest care, lest we violate some of the characteristics of the style.

Our site, then, for an edifice like this, must be somewhat formidable, and have at least the appearance of being able to resist a siege. The interior we find provided with modern improvements, and generally convenient. A door gives entrance to the vestibule from the porch, and this conducts us to the hall. The first door at the right opens into a coat closet; the next communicates with the drawing room. This is elliptical in plan. The boudoir is a cozy apartment, quite retired, and is furnished with a closet. The dining room is of spacious dimensions, and has a large alcove somewhat after the fashion of the Dais, above mentioned, separated from the main apartment by an arch, from which curtains may be hung, thus rendering this Dais or bay sufficiently private for a sitting or music room. This, too, would be an admirable arrangement for tableaux or private theatricals, or, in case of an entertainment, as a practical enlargement of the dining room. The butler's pantry is of good size, communicating by a dumb waiter with the kitchen below. The library is octagonal, having four sides for books, while the others are occupied by doors, windows, and fireplace. There is but one stairway in this house, which extends from the basement to the top of the tower, but so retired that other stairs are deemed unnecessary. The second story contains four large bedrooms, a linen closet and bath room, while the servants' and store rooms are in the attic.

Estimate.—This building, in stone, would cost about $9,500.

Paul Schulze del.

DESIGN No. 26.

THERE is a passion prevalent in our cities, and the rural districts are not wholly exempt from it, for producing the greatest possible show with the least amount of expense. We are well aware that this tendency is generally considered vulgar, and when developed to any great degree, is doubtless open to this imputation; yet in moderation it is but the expression of a considerable self-respect. In building, we think a just amount of this feeling is eminently laudable.

As an illustration, let us suppose a small domain of some two or three acres to have been selected, on which we propose to establish a dwelling, and all the appendages of a small country place. With limited means, we desire to make our place as imposing in appearance as possible, the house itself to be of moderate size, having three rooms and a kitchen on the first floor.   Now, instead of scattering about the grounds the necessary out-buildings, let us group them in such a manner that, taken in connection with the house, they shall each have a value in the *tout ensemble*, and appear of the grand design. We thus have our wood house, shed, carriage house, &c., together, with an enclosed yard for domestic purposes, all apparently forming an extension of the dwelling, and giving our humble house a very desirable degree of dignity and importance, while the position of these subordinate appendages is most convenient.   But should we stop here, we defeat our object; for nothing can be more unbecoming or pretentious than so imposing an array of buildings in so small a domain. We require at least the appearance of a tract of forty or fifty acres, to correspond with the proportions of the building. How shall this be effected? Shall we make the glass of our windows magnifiers? This would do if we were always within doors, but would hardly give the same result from without. The remedy is an easy and natural one. Instead of enclosing your narrow park with a formal fence, standing out in bold relief, and absolutely diminishing by one half the apparent extent of your land, build a stone wall of barely sufficient height to prevent the incursion of cattle; inside this make a bank of earth, sloping gradually from the top of this wall to the ground. This bank you will turf in the same manner as a lawn. Thus the wall is entirely removed from sight, and the adjoining

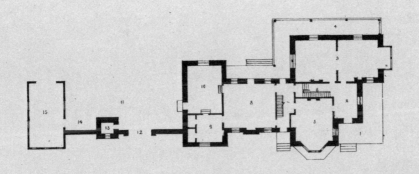

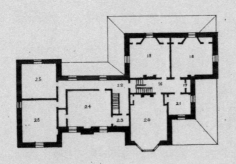

DESIGN Nº 26.

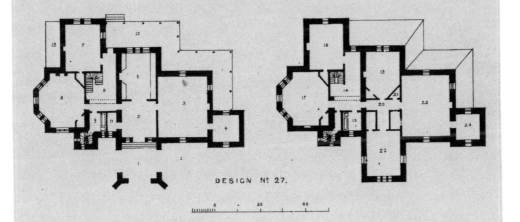

DESIGN Nº 27.

0   20   40

land blends with your own, and appears as much a part and parcel of the whole as if you owned for miles around.

Let us now proceed to a detailed description of the building itself.

As we approach the main entrance, we pass a wide veranda, which communicates with the principal rooms of the ground floor. The main hall is spacious and well lighted, and, being unobstructed by the stairs, might serve the purpose of a sitting room. The drawing rooms are separated by sliding doors, so that one might be used as a library. The dining room has a niche for a sideboard, and a bay window, surrounded outside by a balcony. This room communicates with the kitchen offices by a private entry, which contains a stairway, dresser, butler's sink, &c., and has an exit front and rear. The kitchen is of large proportions, well lighted, and connecting with the wood house and laundry, the latter of which is provided with large pantries and a fireplace. The woodhouse floor is lower than that of the main building, and on a level with the yard, to give greater height for accommodation of stores. The yard before spoken of, is for drying clothes and other domestic purposes, and is concealed by a high wall, provided with a wide gateway, and broken by a lofty, picturesque aviary.

The stable and carriage house, with a room for a man servant in hay loft above, are at the extremity of the group. The advantage of having these appendages thus remote from the house is obvious.

The shed, at No. 14, we would always recommend as an appendage to every country house; for it not only acts as a store place and refuge for fowls, but serves the hospitable purpose of sheltering both horse and carriage of your transient guest.

The chamber accommodations of this house are ample, as it contains seven bed rooms, a bath room and linen closet, while servants' and store rooms may be had in the attic. The kitchen chimney is built on the outside of the house, thus serving to relieve the bareness of the walls, by a pleasing external feature, affording more room for the first and second stories, and excluding the heat in summer.

An objection was raised in Design No. 3 to the finials and ridge ornaments, as serving merely an æsthetical purpose, but here this objection does not obtain, since they are of practical utility. They are of iron, and, bristling with a decorated design, form points for the lightning, and are connected with an ornamental conductor, leading to the ground.

Estimate.—This building, in stone, would cost about $10,500.

DESIGN, N.º 27.

Paul Schulze del.

DESIGN No. 27.

THE reader is now presented with a design, which may be regarded as approaching that of an old English seat, built on a liberal scale. The style adopted is that described in Chap. I., called the Tudor, which was in vogue in England between the reigns of Henry VII. and Elizabeth. This may be considered as the first real development of domestic architecture in England, since, previous to the union of the Houses of York and Lancaster, through the marriage of Henry VII., the fortified castle was the only safe place of residence for either royalty or nobility. When, after years

of internal broils and civil discord, permanent peace was restored
to the nation, the entire mode of life was radically changed, and instead of fortified dwellings, the nobility and gentry began to build
mansions more in accordance with the modern idea of domestic
comfort and elegance. Formidable barriers of rock were no longer
considered the most eligible building sites, but the shady grove,
the gentle slope of lawns and parks, the hill and river side, became
the chosen abodes of the wealth and culture of the nation. The
portcullis and drawbridge were no longer required, the massive
walls were not an imperative necessity ; the loopholes gave place
to windows and bays ; ornaments of convenience and utility made
their appearance, clustering chimneys towered up to the skies ;
porches and oriels adorned the walls, and the roofs were combinations of battlement and gable ; in short, the Tudor style was a
union of all that was beautiful in both castle and abbey.

The main entrance of this design has rather an ecclesiastical
character. The pointed roof and window of the second story is of
the style of the thirteenth century, while the flat arch of the carriage porch and the buttresses which stregthen the piers are of the
fifteenth. The battlemented towers and parapets which here and
there show themselves, partake strongly of the castellated feeling,
and the bay windows, chimneys, &c., may be regarded as new features, peculiar to the Tudor.

As we drive under the porch, which is under a portion of
the second story, we enter a broad and spacious hall, which
communicates by folding doors with the library in the rear. This
library is lighted by a triplet Gothic window, facing the folding
doors. The light coming from but one direction in rooms of
this character, is an advantage of which we have had frequent
occasion to speak. The drawing room is of good size, and connects with a little cabinet used for the purpose of containing curi-

osities, but which may be converted into a private music room. The staircase hall is apart, and communicates with the dining room and bedroom, and has an exit on the rear veranda. The dining room is somewhat octagonal in form, but the fireplace and opposite window recede, so as to give a greater length in this direction. The butler's pantry, which connects with the private staircase, tower, and main stairs, contains a sink, dresser, and dumb waiter, which communicates with the kitchen. A kitchen might be arranged on the first floor, in lieu of the bedroom, communicating with the dining room through its present closet. A kitchen on both floors, in a house of this size, is frequently advisable. The private stairs, above alluded to, extend from the basement, winding through the tower, to the various stories above, and so to the top, which is protected, as will be seen, by the battlement. This roof is of such a height that the views from it, even on ordinary sites, must be very extensive. After ascending the main stairs to the second story hall, we are struck with the spacious apartments so numerous upon this floor.

The bath room and water closet communicate with the hall, and the plumbing of the various stories, which are supplied with water from a tank in the attic, is economized by the exact superimposition of the apartments in which it is used. The billiard room and spare chambers are arranged in the attic, where sufficient height of ceiling is obtained, without infringing on a large space between the ceiling and roof, which is designed to prevent the direct action of the weather, and to give good air for the rooms below, whose ventilating shafts terminate in this space, and all pass through an " Emerson ventilator " above the roof.

The view given of this house is taken from a point in front, where the verandas, which are all in the rear, are not seen. The reason of this is, the exposure and view from the front are not particularly desirable, while in the rear they are peculiarly so.

The material of this house would naturally be stone; yet if that is not of convenient access, brick or stucco would not be objectionable; but wood is not in any case adapted to this style of architecture, as its details are designed only for masonry.

Ivy or other vines are always appropriate for the ornamenting of the Gothic, and add much to its picturesqueness. As the English ivy is not a hardy plant in our country, the Virginia creeper is often substituted with good effect. Its only disadvantage is that it is not an evergreen; yet it leaves out early in the Spring, and is in constant verdure until late in Autumn, when it is changed by frost into the most gorgeous tints imaginable. The English ivy in some localities has, even in our coldest exposures, been made to thrive and grow vigorously, as at the residence of the late Washington Irving, where the ivy literally covers one side of the house.

It will be found advantageous, in cultivating this vine, to plant it on the north side of the house, where, after it has been touched by frost, it is not immediately exposed to the sun, which is often the greater enemy of the two. It needs but little heat, and considerable humidity of atmosphere, as in England.

Estimate.—This building, in stone, would cost about $28,000.

Paul Schulze, del.

Print by H. Lawrence, 83, William St. N.Y.

DESIGN Nº 28.

DESIGN No. 28.

ALTERATIONS of old buildings, when extensive, are not usually considered advisable, as the cost of much alteration is nearly, if not quite, equal to that of an entirely new edifice. Another serious objection is the embarrassment usually attending the fixed lines of the original structure, which limit the architect to a narrow field for the display of whatever ability he may possess. Yet it frequently happens that a family have already on their land a decent dwelling, endeared by many associations, whose total destruction would seem almost sacrilegious, as well as wanton waste of property. Either a new field must be sought for the desired improvements, or we must alter the present mansion; and the latter is the usual and perhaps more natural course.

This is no easy task for the architect, who, when a double labor has been expended, and but a partial effect produced, may well shrink from that paternal responsibility which otherwise he would readily have .assumed, and deprecate the criticism which, under other circumstances, he would gladly have invited.

The accompanying design will somewhat illustrate how far we have been successful in the alteration of a moderately sized dwelling, which was the residence of Geo. A. Hoyt, Esq., of Stamford, Conn. The original building, which may be seen in the vignette at the right of the ground plan, was finely situated within an enclosure of some half dozen acres, shaded by deciduous trees. The building was of stone, and of so substantial a character and so well arranged, that the owner wisely concluded that alteration would be better than tearing down and building anew. In the plan of the first story, the dark portion represents the old house, and the lighter the additions.

The original arrangement was preserved so far as was practicable. The drawing room, which was added, being much larger than the other rooms, it was thought should have a greater height of ceiling than the rest of the house, and this caused a discrepancy of some four feet between the roofs. Some difficulty was anticipated in the management of this room to obtain sufficient size, as we were unable to extend it more than twenty feet from the house, and the rear wall was fixed by the position of the dining room windows. Not wishing to cut off the light, it was decided to extend the addition ten feet in front, and thus, by the aid of a large bay window, sufficient room was obtained. Again, the library and chamber above were too small. How else could we enlarge them than by extending them in the same manner? We cannot have a bay window in the library, as it would project into the road leading to the carriage porch; but this room is now large enough, and the trouble is with the bedroom above. This must be increased in size; but how shall it be effected? The idea suggests itself

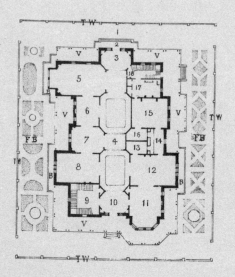

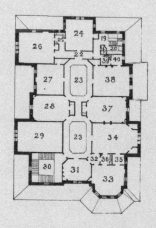

DESIGN No 29.

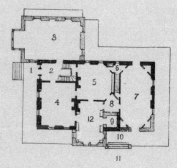

DESIGN No 28.

that a bay window may be placed in the second story, not extending to the ground, but supported by brackets, forming what may be called an oriel. Now that we have an interior of sufficient size, how shall we treat these awkward projections without? It occurs to us that we require an observatory, as no extended view can be had from the lower rooms, and the view in the distance is fine. We will therefore run the library projection above the roof and form a tower. This we will furnish with a railing, that we may mount to the very summit. Thus we relieve the discrepancy in height of the drawing room roof, which made the house look one-sided and unsymmetrical. Now we have obtained a balance of parts; and the irregularity of the roof gives the whole design a distinctive and decided character, and a broken and picturesque skyline.

The French chateau roof, which we have adopted, gives ample space for servants' apartments and other necessary rooms in the attic, and, by the flat on top, furnishes a means of collecting water for the tank, and provides a place on which we may walk, surrounded, as it is, with an iron railing for protection. We have provided, also, that the projections of the drawing room and library shall be just sufficient to receive the veranda, which extends along the front and sides of the house, and fills up the vacancy between. We now discover that the veranda around the saloon excludes the light from the kitchen, which is directly beneath it. Here is an unforeseen difficulty. We must have this veranda, and the location of the kitchen cannot be changed. We have seen in the city large blocks of glass let into the floor, that the light from a skylight above may pass through to the story below. This idea we adopt. That part of the veranda floor directly over each window in the kitchen we make of this thick glass, and are gratified to find that our experiment is entirely successful.

Paul Schulze del.

Print by H. Lawrence 83 William St. N.Y.

DESIGN Nº 29.

DESIGN No. 29.

THIS villa was designed for a wealthy gentleman, who has recently purchased one of the most charming sites on the shores of
the Sound. The grounds are of some years' standing, and were
laid out by one of the best landscape gardeners in the country.
They are covered with the choicest kinds of evergreen and deciduous trees, so arranged as to enhance the natural beauties of the
place. The estate has lately been much improved by the introduction of artificial waters in fountains, lakes, and streams, with
the usual concomitants of aquatic birds and plants, arbors, bridges,
and pleasure boats. The roads are well made, and wind gracefully
among groves and lawns, and by the water side, in such a manner
as to deceive the eye, and cause the small park of fifty acres to
seem double that size.

It is pleasant to note this growing disposition among our
wealthy citizens to cultivate the refinements of rural beauties. In
our cities we often find sums lavished on palatial residences, sufficient to build a host of villas in the country, and yet the effect
of such lavish expenditure is comparatively lost amid so much tedious repetition of design. It seems to us a marked indication
of wisdom and good taste, instead of expending a princely amount
on a narrow plot of ground in some aristocratic quarter of the
city, to establish an elegant and independent country seat, at a less
actual outlay, with gardens and pleasure grounds, and all those
elegant appliances of a luxurious rural home, which, while they
delight and give occupation to the mind, do not, like the dissipations of the city, debauch the body and undermine the health. To
be " monarch of all he surveys," in the midst of the fine repose and
healthy ease of an estate in the country, is the unfailing desire of
every man who has resources within himself against *ennui*, and
large capacities to develop in the paths of elegant culture. It may
be said that such a home as we have pictured is a luxury too ex-

pensive to be dreamed of save by few. Such is not the case to the extent generally supposed. The difference in taxes alone between town and country would defray the extra expense of maintaining the grounds, and the many economical advantages of a country life have been too often dwelt upon to need recapitulation here.

The exterior of this house, which is strictly Italian, and in harmony with the scenery amid which it is placed, is intended to convey the sentiments of refined household comfort and repose, and of a large and noble hospitality. The architecture being rather of a grave and formal character, it seems necessary to separate it somewhat from the easy slopes and natural grace of the lawns and banks around, by a broad terrace, which acts as a base to the building, and prepares the mind for the comparative severity of its lines. By referring to the ground plan, it will be observed that on two sides of the house the carriage road occupies the space between the terrace wall and the house, while on the other sides this space is occupied by flower beds, statuary, and fountains. The introduction of these latter features upon the lawn would produce an incongruous effect, they being too precise and formal for such a position. But this objection does not attach to their present location, where the object is to establish a connection between the severity of architecture and the easy, natural grace of nature. While the advantage of such artificial ornaments, as seen from the windows and balconies, is obvious, yet they form but a foreground to the wider extent of the park and woodland beyond.

The carriage porch is unusually large, being long enough to shelter both carriage and horses. The veranda and balconies, which are very wide, extend quite around the house, forming a walk of several hundred feet. The ceilings of the first story are twenty feet high, and the extreme width of the main hall is the same. This hall has two large openings (23, 23) in the ceiling, extending through the second story to the roof, where there are domes surrounded by skylights.

The drawing room, boudoir, music, and billiard rooms supply a vista through the house by the opening of folding doors, while the dining room, hall, and billiard room may be connected in the same manner. The billiard room, also used as a picture gallery, extends up to the roof, and has a railed balcony between the openings (23, 29). This room is lighted from above, and also at the side, by a high triplet window, which may be regulated by shades.

The dining room communicates with the kitchen by a large butler's pantry, the laundry with the linen closet on the second story, and the drying room in the attic by a dumb waiter. The second story contains nine sleeping apartments, all large, and most of them connected with bath and dressing rooms. The grand staircase occupies the entire tower, and extends to the observatory, while, at the other end of the hall, are other stairs of less pretensions, extending to the attic, which is divided into good apartments for servants' and store rooms.

Estimate.—This building, in brick, would cost about $45,000.

DESIGN

Paul Schulze del.

Print by H. Lawrence, 83 William St. N. Y.

DESIGN No. 30.

Of city architecture but little has been said, because it is not strictly within the province of this work. There is, however, one phase of this architecture which recommends itself to our notice, as embodying many of those principles which we have repeatedly enumerated with reference to rural architecture, such as a more careful distribution of masses and a nicer study of extensive skylines with reference to block designs as seen from a distance. In building on open spaces or parks, a proper observance of these principles is essential to elegance and artistic effect.

Though our streets are lined for miles of their extent with expensive buildings, their general perspective effect is so unsatisfactory that the stranger, for the first time in New York, is puzzled and embarrassed to find out the system on which we build. Probably there is no city in the world having streets as extensive as our Broadway and Fifth Avenue, adorned with the same amount of pretentious and costly architecture; but still the result is less pleasing than that in some streets of European towns, whose buildings are of a much plainer character. The reason of this is our total disregard of harmony. Our designs are often elaborate, and sometimes beautiful, yet, as they rarely have an opportunity for fully expressing themselves, but are usually confined to one or two city lots, and as they are likely to be elbowed by uncongenial

buildings on either side, the character of whose lines may materially obviate or entirely cancel that of our own, the general result
is like the *disjecta membra poetœ*, chaotic, disconnected, and discordant.

These are defects which can scarcely be remedied where they
already exist, but which should be avoided in future erections.
Especially should they be regarded in the construction of those
buildings which are to spring up around our parks. Occupying
sites so conspicuous, these blocks should be carefully studied in
masses and outline, so that each house may not be entirely independent and individual as now, but a responsible part of a general
design. This can only be effected by an agreement of all the parties proposing to build in the block, or by care being taken that
each successive house, as it is erected, may form an harmonious
union with those which have preceded it. It is not meant that all
should build alike—far from it; since irregularity, with a due attention to harmony, is an important source of beauty in architecture. One roof may tower above another, neighboring houses may
vary in height of stories or size or fashion of apertures, without
being necessarily discordant one with another. It is only essential
that these differences should be so managed as to combine with
mutual advantage, so that no part of a block may seem to be acci-
dental or intrusive.

Houses around parks may be viewed from a distance, where
details are not visible, and their beauty must therefore in great
part consist in a judicious grouping of the several buildings in the
block to produce some general design. What would be the appearance from the middle of a park of a block composed of eight
separate and distinct styles of architecture, bearing no relation to
each other—one tall, another short, one wide, another narrow, one
with horizontal lines predominating, another with perpendicular

lines predominating, one ornate, another bare, and so on? Would it not remind one of the marshalling of the army of Falstaff?

In a narrow street, where we can do little more than examine from a near point the details of each façade, the general design of a whole block is not of so much importance; but in blocks fronting on an open square, it is not sufficient that each component house should be irreproachable as regards detail, but it should so harmonize with its neighbors that the whole would be a case of *E pluribus unum*, from which secession would be equivalent to dissolution.

What would be the result were the grand Park, which is to be the pride not only of our city, but of the entire country, a field for the disconnected operations of fifty different architects, each following his own design, without reference to the others? Each might have merit in his invention, yet, without a proper mutual understanding, the entire effect would be absurd, and a result attained inferior to what the most unworthy among them might have accomplished, if left to himself.

Extensive property holders or speculators, who build an entire block, may carry throughout, of course, any design they prefer. It is to be regretted that they make use of this privilege not to create a *unity* of design, but rather a *uniformity*—a weary and monotonous repetition of general features and details, the whole having the appearance of cheap contract work turned out with a machine, and the unfortunate purchaser, in the middle of such a block, can only recognize his own house by his name on the doorplate, or by the color of his curtains.

The design we offer is an attempt to prove that houses of different heights and of different degrees of finish and costliness, may be put together so as to produce a harmonious whole. Obviously, it is the duty of architects, when, as is usually the case, they are

called upon to *sandwich* a house from between obstinate and stiff-
necked neighbors, with windows of different heights, built of different materials, and with discordant lines, to act as a peacemaker,
and do all he can with his own design to reconcile all these painful
differences. The task is a difficult one, and the architect's skill is
scarcely recognized by the public. But the problem is given, and
it is for architects to solve it as best they can.

Other governments have seen fit to legislate upon the subject
of street architecture with the happiest results, and though certainly sumptuary laws of this kind are not with us advisable, yet
we have sometimes dreamed that architectural harmony might be
encouraged by offering certain privileges, as a temporary reduction
of taxes, to those who will submit their plans to the censorship of
a public officer, chosen by architects, whose duty it shall be to observe certain approved æsthetic standards of design of generous
and not tyrannical application, as well as to preside over the operations of the laws for protection against unsafe buildings.

Paul Schulze del.

Print. by H. Lawrence, 83 William St. N. Y.

DESIGN No. 31.

In our country, utility and ugliness seem to be almost synonymous terms. It is not understood that a useful object may be made beautiful, not only without destroying its utility, but even adding to it. For one of the great sources of beauty is fitness, and it has been observed that all those implements, whether of mechanism or husbandry, which are best suited for the purposes to which they are applied, are the most graceful and pleasing in form.

Perhaps no object suffers so much, from a total disregard to this principle, as the saw mills of our country. They always, from necessity, occupy the wildest and most picturesque localities, where the best water-power can be obtained, and so unworthy are they usually to associate with such scenes, that we are in the habit of considering them nuisances and desecrations. We have endeavored to show in our sketch that such buildings need not necessarily be an offensive intrusion into the wild scenery where they belong. It needs but a judicious emphasis of those necessary features which may add to its picturesqueness of outline, such as irregularity of roof, dormers and apertures of varying shapes, together with an artistic adjustment of great beams and foundation piers, so as to enter happily into the composition. Actually, such careful adjustment of parts need not add to the expense of the building, or in the slightest degree interfere with its usefulness.

But the rustic design which we present was scarcely intended to serve any legitimate purpose of practical utility. It is the proposed remodelling of an old dilapidated mill, which happened to stand within the grounds of an extensive estate belonging to a wealthy proprietor, and which, instead of being suffered to fall to decay, was thought worthy of applying to uses not contemplated in its original intentions.

With a slight outlay, such a structure may be converted to various purposes of pleasure, while it may be made to harmonize happily with the scenery amidst which it stands. The old bridge, with its shed, which in bygone days served for the protection of the farmer's load of corn, may now shelter the saddle horses of a pleasure party on a sultry day. The first floor may serve as a summer house, a noonday resort for the family. The second floor may be used as a billiard room. Even the wheels may be preserved, and, as the water privilege is as good as ever, it may be used to work the force pump connected with a reservoir, from which may be obtained the household supply of water, and which may furnish a head for the fountains in the garden. The reservoir tower, too, may form another agreeable feature in the landscape, and from its elevated position may serve also as an observatory. In an estate like this, of one or two hundred acres, abundant resources for every amusement are embraced. Rural sports of all kinds may be enjoyed without leaving the grounds, and here the family, after the winter campaign of city life, and perhaps a brief dissipation at the watering places, may live as quiet and independent as if nothing of the world's follies could ever enter within the gates.

Print. by H. Lawrence, 83, William St. N.Y.

Paul Schulze del.

DESIGN Nº 32.

DESIGN No. 32.

SOME of the most pleasing and poetic ideas of our literature have arisen from associations connected with unpretending rural churches. Every person capable of sympathizing with these sentiments will at once perceive the importance of allowing them to exercise a large influence over the construction of every such building. It is from a continual and systematic disregard of these poetic associations that have arisen that vacancy and coldness of sentiment which distinguish most of our parish chapels and " meeting houses."

On a Sabbath morning, after the toil and cares of the week, spent, perhaps, in the town, and quite worn out by fatigue and heat, we involuntarily find consolation and pleasant greeting in the sweet sounds of " the church-going bells." Gently the melodious strains fall from the modest spire and echo among the hills. Our steps are irresistibly drawn churchward. The village meeting house is nearer, and attended by a more fashionable audience, but we

have seen enough of such worship, and long for a participation in
that of a simpler and purer tone.   So our first glance at the plain
and almost severe architecture of this little church gives us a sen-
sation of relief, and we feel that this indeed is " the house of God."
We draw nearer by the winding roads, and at length reach the
litch gate, that gives entrance into the churchyard.   Here, shaded
by noble trees, and among moss-covered gravestones, " the rude
forefathers of the hamlet sleep."

> " Yet e'en these bones from insult to protect,
>   Some frail memorial still erected nigh,
>   With uncouth rhymes and shapeless sculpture decked,
>   Implores the passing tribute of a sigh."

Hard by stands the church.   The ivy has crept quite up its
rugged walls, and, undisturbed and undirected, invested them with
tokens of the tender sympathy of nature.   As we enter, we instinctively and reverently bow.   As without, so within, all is plain
and, it may be, rude, yet so strictly appropriate that the very air
seems holy.

Let us turn from this quiet picture, and compare with it that
much more frequent one of the pretentious and formal place of
worship, which doubtless is a characteristic of our country.   It
stands in a cramped and unattractive spot, given, probably, by
some worldly-minded parishioner, who, as he gave, estimated the
sure rise in his surrounding land.   A lumber merchant, a carpenter, and a " solid man " constitute the building committee.   The
material selected is wood, of course, that it may be furnished by
the lumber merchant, and the carpenter make a good profit on the
contract, while the plan adopted is that most pleasing to our " solid man," from whom a liberal donation is expected.   This is not
an overdrawn picture, but only too truly indicates the manner in

which many of our churches are built. Frequently, stone designs are built in wood, sanded, and blocked off most cunningly. The interior walls of plaster must also represent stone, and the really respectable furniture of wood must be painted in imitation of some more expensive material.

There can be no greater inconsistency than these continual expressions of falsehood, in a place which should, of all others, be devoted to truth. If compelled, from a scarcity of stone, or other cause, to employ wood, let your churches show a wood construction; if your interior walls are of plaster, so let them appear, appropriately ornamented, if you will, but never deceptive.

The interior of the design we present is bold but simple. The north entrance porch is balanced by a similar structure on the south, which is used for the organ and choir, thus carrying out the cruciform plan. The principal feature is the deep and spacious chancel, which not only always adds great effect to the design, but gives solemnity to the services of the church.

In regard to the bell, it may be necessary to state that the rope should pass through a pipe built in the wall and terminating in the vestry room, otherwise it would hang awkwardly before the chancel.

Estimate.—The above design would cost about $6,000. The author has recently furnished similar designs for a church at Wilton, Conn., to cost $4,500, with 350 sittings.

Print by H. Lawrence, 83, William St. N.Y.

Paul Schulze del.

DESIGN No. 33.

WE have frequently been asked why Catholic places of worship, and especially those of the Church of England, generally present an appearance so much more pleasing than those of other denominations. What is the secret of that graceful gravity, that "beauty of holiness," which so distinguishes the churches and chapels of the Romish and the "Established" faiths? From the time of Constantine until the Reformation, the Christian architects, inspired by the idea of making a visible religion, of rendering the material church an exponent of the spiritual church, studied very deeply the æsthetical significance of form, and embodied the results of their researches in the most impressive series of buildings the world has ever seen. They seemed to amalgamate matter and spirit into a vast system of symbolism, which exercised a despotic sway over the art of architecture, not only in decorative details, but in the general plans and outlines. It was not unnatural, therefore, that the Lutheran Reformers should regard with great distrust a style of architecture which seemed to have arisen from the Popish Ritual, and to be full of the emotional wiles and strategies of the corrupt church. After the Reformation, the feeling became so strong against the abuses of Rome that, in the anxiety to throw off all her evils, they discarded many good points, and among these, her grand and beautiful symbolic architecture.

The Church of England, however, less radical than the other branches of Protestantism, within the present century has discovered this error, repaired her dilapidated cathedrals, and revived in her parish churches the pure styles of bygone ages.

The accompanying design, which was intended for a country parish church, is of the style of the fourteenth century, as described in Chap. I. The plan is cruciform, and the chancel window looks toward the East, thus preserving the two leading symbols of the mediæval churches, and commemorating the birth and death of our Saviour. If we build for the worship of God, our building should be worthy of its sacred object. Doubtless, a lavish introduction of symbols, as such, without any practical advantage attached to them, would not be consistent with the prejudices of many modern Christians; but we wish to show that many of these emblems originally had a no less definite use than signification. With respect to the cruciform plan, for instance, it is always necessary in public auditoriums to bring the audience as near as possible to the speaker. Now, as, in the accompanying design, the proportions of the roof limit the width of the nave, and the distance from the chancel limits its length, we are obliged to add wings or transepts. These, if placed near the chancel, with their galleries, bring the greater part of the congregation near it. We have also in this design extended the nave laterally by the aid of low aisles.

To give light and ventilation to the upper part of the church, we introduce gablet windows, which supply the place of the more costly clerestory windows, and a lantern ventilator upon the roof. All these, it will be noticed, also act as æsthetic features, serving to break up the bareness and length of the roof, and give piquancy to the general lines.

If a chimney is required in the church, we should not hesitate to show it, only the detailed treatment should be harmonious with the general design. Such an one we have endeavored to show on the right of this sketch.

Estimate.—The above design would cost about $15,000.

Paul Schulze del.

DESIGN Nº 34.

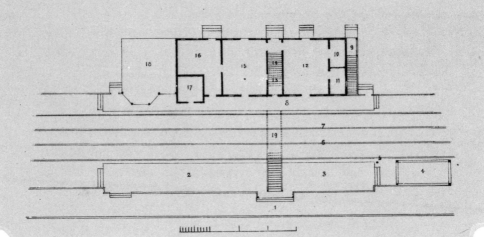

DESIGN No. 34.

It is now received as an axiom in modern political economy, that the construction of railways from large cities through the rural districts not only must increase the population and industry of such districts, but must act as most effective agents of social reform. The natural overflow of the city into the country necessarily carries with it an element of refinement and culture, so that we find society, in every village which is touched by a railroad, slowly and surely improving, as is plainly shown in the vanishing of old Puritan, Dutch, or Quaker prejudices in the matter of architecture, before the healthy example of the rusticating citizen, who builds his elegant villa or picturesque cottage in their neighborhood.   It is certainly reasonable to suppose that railway companies themselves, being thus the great modern *civilizing* instruments, would be foremost in setting examples of improved taste and culture before the people, by building stations along their lines, which should be agreeable objects to look upon, and stand as models of design.   Such seed, though sown by the wayside, would not be entirely lost, but would surely bear its fruits in the increased refinement of rural sentiment, and the greater demand for country places along the lines of railway routes. Usually, however, these railway stations, even on our most prominent roads, are of the most uninviting or even ridiculous appearance.   When they are not beggarly, they are often absurdly pretentious.   We remember seeing a frequented railway station fashioned somewhat after the manner of a hugh Egyptian temple, with the fuel house near by imitated from the towering Pylon, *yet all built most palpably and painfully of boards!* We are glad to note, however, that in some individual instances an evidence of an improved taste and a more refined feeling for elegance or propriety is shown.   We wish that the stranger, entering an American town or village, were welcomed by something more inviting than those rude sheds under which he shakes off the dust of travel.

Perhaps nothing more readily attracts the attention of the American traveller than the beautiful little stations which, with endless variety, are dotted along the railway web of Great Britain and the continent.   There railway travelling is a luxury, not only in the assurance of safety, and the splendid fitting of the carriages, but in the tasteful little stations which not only charm the eye by their agreeable exteriors, but comfort the weariness of journeying by their convenient and perfect arrangement within.   In our country such a mode of conveyance involves somewhat of personal danger, as the lists of casualties assure us, and the eye is constantly offended by those unworthy structures which we dignify with the name of stations.

We by no means advocate extensive or expensive buildings for wayside stations, but, on the contrary, merely convenient and economical arrangements, with a large amount of that inexpensive commodity—*taste*. Considerations of safety, we think, should exercise more influence over the designing and placing of these structures, and the management of their surroundings. In no other country do we find the rails so exposed, so subject to the intrusion of cattle and other obstructions, with carriage roads crossing the track, unguarded by gates or bridges. Many valuable lives have been lost from the necessity of crossing the track to enter the station. Travellers from abroad look aghast at such wanton carelessness, while we, with our go-ahead propensities, think nothing of it, and take no measures to prevent such accidents.

In the present design we have endeavored to obviate some of the faults alluded to. Here, it will be observed, it is unnecessary for persons to cross the tracks, a bridge being provided, to enable travellers to cross from one side to the other of the rails without danger. Thus direct entrances are obtained into the station from both sides of the tracks. The rails are protected by an outside fence. The cross roads should either be bridged or protected by gates, which should be closed across the road when a train is expected, and at other times across the rails, to prevent the entrance of cattle.

THE END.

A CATALOG OF SELECTED
DOVER BOOKS
IN ALL FIELDS OF INTEREST

A CATALOG OF SELECTED
DOVER BOOKS
IN ALL FIELDS OF INTEREST

DRAWINGS OF REMBRANDT, edited by Seymour Slive. Updated Lippmann, Hofstede de Groot edition, with definitive scholarly apparatus. All portraits, biblical sketches, landscapes, nudes. Oriental figures, classical studies, together with selection of work by followers. 550 illustrations. Total of 630pp. 9⅛ × 12¼.
21485-0, 21486-9 Pa., Two-vol. set $29.90

GHOST AND HORROR STORIES OF AMBROSE BIERCE, Ambrose Bierce. 24 tales vividly imagined, strangely prophetic, and decades ahead of their time in technical skill: "The Damned Thing," "An Inhabitant of Carcosa," "The Eyes of the Panther," "Moxon's Master," and 20 more. 199pp. 5⅜ × 8½.   20767-6 Pa. $4.95

ETHICAL WRITINGS OF MAIMONIDES, Maimonides. Most significant ethical works of great medieval sage, newly translated for utmost precision, readability. Laws Concerning Character Traits, Eight Chapters, more. 192pp. 5⅜ × 8½.
24522-5 Pa. $5.95

THE EXPLORATION OF THE COLORADO RIVER AND ITS CANYONS, J. W. Powell. Full text of Powell's 1,000-mile expedition down the fabled Colorado in 1869. Superb account of terrain, geology, vegetation, Indians, famine, mutiny, treacherous rapids, mighty canyons, during exploration of last unknown part of continental U.S. 400pp. 5⅜ × 8½.   20094-9 Pa. $8.95

HISTORY OF PHILOSOPHY, Julián Marías. Clearest one-volume history on the market. Every major philosopher and dozens of others, to Existentialism and later. 505pp. 5⅜ × 8½.   21739-6 Pa. $9.95

ALL ABOUT LIGHTNING, Martin A. Uman. Highly readable nontechnical survey of nature and causes of lightning, thunderstorms, ball lightning, St. Elmo's Fire, much more. Illustrated. 192pp. 5⅜ × 8½.   25237-X Pa. $5.95

SAILING ALONE AROUND THE WORLD, Captain Joshua Slocum. First man to sail around the world, alone, in small boat. One of great feats of seamanship told in delightful manner. 67 illustrations. 294pp. 5⅜ × 8½.   20326-3 Pa. $4.95

LETTERS AND NOTES ON THE MANNERS, CUSTOMS AND CONDITIONS OF THE NORTH AMERICAN INDIANS, George Catlin. Classic account of life among Plains Indians: ceremonies, hunt, warfare, etc. 312 plates. 572pp. of text. 6⅛ × 9¼.   22118-0, 22119-9, Pa., Two-vol. set $17.90

THE SECRET LIFE OF SALVADOR DALÍ, Salvador Dalí. Outrageous but fascinating autobiography through Dalí's thirties with scores of drawings and sketches and 80 photographs. A must for lovers of 20th-century art. 432pp. 6½ × 9¼. (Available in U.S. only)   27454-3 Pa. $9.95

ILLUSTRATED GUIDE TO SHAKER FURNITURE, Robert Meader. All furniture and appurtenances, with much on unknown local styles. 235 photos. 146pp. 9 × 12. 22819-3 Pa. $9.95

WHALE SHIPS AND WHALING: A Pictorial Survey, George Francis Dow. Over 200 vintage engravings, drawings, photographs of barks, brigs, cutters, other vessels. Also harpoons, lances, whaling guns, many other artifacts. Comprehensive text by foremost authority. 207 black-and-white illustrations. 288pp. 6 × 9. 24808-9 Pa. $9.95

THE BERTRAMS, Anthony Trollope. Powerful portrayal of blind self-will and thwarted ambition includes one of Trollope's most heartrending love stories. 497pp. 5⅜ × 8½. 25119-5 Pa. $9.95

ADVENTURES WITH A HAND LENS, Richard Headstrom. Clearly written guide to observing and studying flowers and grasses, fish scales, moth and insect wings, egg cases, buds, feathers, seeds, leaf scars, moss, molds, ferns, common crystals, etc.—all with an ordinary, inexpensive magnifying glass. 209 exact line drawings aid in your discoveries. 220pp. 5⅜ × 8½. 23330-8 Pa. $5.95

RODIN ON ART AND ARTISTS, Auguste Rodin. Great sculptor's candid, wide-ranging comments on meaning of art; great artists; relation of sculpture to poetry, painting, music; philosophy of life, more. 76 superb black-and-white illustrations of Rodin's sculpture, drawings and prints. 119pp. 8⅜ × 11¼. 24487-3 Pa. $7.95

FIFTY CLASSIC FRENCH FILMS, 1912-1982: A Pictorial Record, Anthony Slide. Memorable stills from Grand Illusion, Beauty and the Beast, Hiroshima, Mon Amour, many more. Credits, plot synopses, reviews, etc. 160pp. 8¼ × 11. 25256-6 Pa. $11.95

THE PRINCIPLES OF PSYCHOLOGY, William James. Famous long course complete, unabridged. Stream of thought, time perception, memory, experimental methods; great work decades ahead of its time. 94 figures. 1,391pp. 5⅜ × 8½. 20381-6, 20382-4 Pa., Two-vol. set $25.90

BODIES IN A BOOKSHOP, R. T. Campbell. Challenging mystery of blackmail and murder with ingenious plot and superbly drawn characters. In the best tradition of British suspense fiction. 192pp. 5⅜ × 8½. 24720-1 Pa. $5.95

CALLAS: Portrait of a Prima Donna, George Jellinek. Renowned commentator on the musical scene chronicles incredible career and life of the most controversial, fascinating, influential operatic personality of our time. 64 black-and-white photographs. 416pp. 5⅜ × 8¼. 25047-4 Pa. $8.95

GEOMETRY, RELATIVITY AND THE FOURTH DIMENSION, Rudolph Rucker. Exposition of fourth dimension, concepts of relativity as Flatland characters continue adventures. Popular, easily followed yet accurate, profound. 141 illustrations. 133pp. 5⅜ × 8½. 23400-2 Pa. $4.95

HOUSEHOLD STORIES BY THE BROTHERS GRIMM, with pictures by Walter Crane. 53 classic stories—Rumpelstiltskin, Rapunzel, Hansel and Gretel, the Fisherman and his Wife, Snow White, Tom Thumb, Sleeping Beauty, Cinderella, and so much more—lavishly illustrated with original 19th-century drawings. 114 illustrations. x + 269pp. 5⅜ × 8½. 21080-4 Pa. $4.95

THE BLUE FAIRY BOOK, Andrew Lang. The first, most famous collection, with many familiar tales: Little Red Riding Hood, Aladdin and the Wonderful Lamp, Puss in Boots, Sleeping Beauty, Hansel and Gretel, Rumpelstiltskin; 37 in all. 138 illustrations. 390pp. 5⅜ × 8½. 21437-0 Pa. $6.95

THE STORY OF THE CHAMPIONS OF THE ROUND TABLE, Howard Pyle. Sir Launcelot, Sir Tristram and Sir Percival in spirited adventures of love and triumph retold in Pyle's inimitable style. 50 drawings, 31 full-page. xviii + 329pp. 6½ × 9¼. 21883-X Pa. $7.95

THE MYTHS OF THE NORTH AMERICAN INDIANS, Lewis Spence. Myths and legends of the Algonquins, Iroquois, Pawnees and Sioux with comprehensive historical and ethnological commentary. 36 illustrations. 5⅜ × 8½.
25967-6 Pa. $8.95

GREAT DINOSAUR HUNTERS AND THEIR DISCOVERIES, Edwin H. Colbert. Fascinating, lavishly illustrated chronicle of dinosaur research, 1820s to 1960. Achievements of Cope, Marsh, Brown, Buckland, Mantell, Huxley, many others. 384pp. 5¼ × 8¼. 24701-5 Pa. $8.95

THE TASTEMAKERS, Russell Lynes. Informal, illustrated social history of American taste 1850s–1950s. First popularized categories Highbrow, Lowbrow, Middlebrow. 129 illustrations. New (1979) afterword. 384pp. 6 × 9.
23993-4 Pa. $8.95

NORTH AMERICAN INDIAN LIFE: Customs and Traditions of 23 Tribes, Elsie Clews Parsons (ed.). 27 fictionalized essays by noted anthropologists examine religion, customs, government, additional facets of life among the Winnebago, Crow, Zuni, Eskimo, other tribes. 480pp. 6⅛ × 9¼. 27377-6 Pa. $10.95

AUTHENTIC VICTORIAN DECORATION AND ORNAMENTATION IN FULL COLOR: 46 Plates from "Studies in Design," Christopher Dresser. Superb full-color lithographs reproduced from rare original portfolio of a major Victorian designer. 48pp. 9¼ × 12¼. 25083-0 Pa. $7.95

PRIMITIVE ART, Franz Boas. Remains the best text ever prepared on subject, thoroughly discussing Indian, African, Asian, Australian, and, especially, Northern American primitive art. Over 950 illustrations show ceramics, masks, totem poles, weapons, textiles, paintings, much more. 376pp. 5⅜ × 8. 20025-6 Pa. $8.95

SIDELIGHTS ON RELATIVITY, Albert Einstein. Unabridged republication of two lectures delivered by the great physicist in 1920–21. *Ether and Relativity* and *Geometry and Experience*. Elegant ideas in nonmathematical form, accessible to intelligent layman. vi + 56pp. 5⅜ × 8½. 24511-X Pa. $3.95

THE WIT AND HUMOR OF OSCAR WILDE, edited by Alvin Redman. More than 1,000 ripostes, paradoxes, wisecracks: Work is the curse of the drinking classes, I can resist everything except temptation, etc. 258pp. 5⅜ × 8½. 20602-5 Pa. $4.95

ADVENTURES WITH A MICROSCOPE, Richard Headstrom. 59 adventures with clothing fibers, protozoa, ferns and lichens, roots and leaves, much more. 142 illustrations. 232pp. 5⅜ × 8½. 23471-1 Pa. $4.95

AMERICAN CLIPPER SHIPS: 1833–1858, Octavius T. Howe & Frederick C. Matthews. Fully-illustrated, encyclopedic review of 352 clipper ships from the period of America's greatest maritime supremacy. Introduction. 109 halftones. 5 black-and-white line illustrations. Index. Total of 928pp. 5⅜ × 8½.
25115-2, 25116-0 Pa., Two-vol. set $21.90

TOWARDS A NEW ARCHITECTURE, Le Corbusier. Pioneering manifesto by great architect, near legendary founder of "International School." Technical and aesthetic theories, views on industry, economics, relation of form to function, "mass-production spirit," much more. Profusely illustrated. Unabridged translation of 13th French edition. Introduction by Frederick Etchells. 320pp. 6⅛ × 9¼. (Available in U.S. only)
25023-7 Pa. $8.95

THE BOOK OF KELLS, edited by Blanche Cirker. Inexpensive collection of 32 full-color, full-page plates from the greatest illuminated manuscript of the Middle Ages, painstakingly reproduced from rare facsimile edition. Publisher's Note. Captions. 32pp. 9⅜ × 12¼. (Available in U.S. only)
24345-1 Pa. $5.95

BEST SCIENCE FICTION STORIES OF H. G. WELLS, H. G. Wells. Full novel *The Invisible Man*, plus 17 short stories: "The Crystal Egg," "Aepyornis Island," "The Strange Orchid," etc. 303pp. 5⅜ × 8½. (Available in U.S. only)
21531-8 Pa. $6.95

AMERICAN SAILING SHIPS: Their Plans and History, Charles G. Davis. Photos, construction details of schooners, frigates, clippers, other sailcraft of 18th to early 20th centuries—plus entertaining discourse on design, rigging, nautical lore, much more. 137 black-and-white illustrations. 240pp. 6⅛ × 9¼.
24658-2 Pa. $6.95

ENTERTAINING MATHEMATICAL PUZZLES, Martin Gardner. Selection of author's favorite conundrums involving arithmetic, money, speed, etc., with lively commentary. Complete solutions. 112pp. 5⅜ × 8½.
25211-6 Pa. $3.95

THE WILL TO BELIEVE, HUMAN IMMORTALITY, William James. Two books bound together. Effect of irrational on logical, and arguments for human immortality. 402pp. 5⅜ × 8½.
20291-7 Pa. $8.95

THE HAUNTED MONASTERY and THE CHINESE MAZE MURDERS, Robert Van Gulik. 2 full novels by Van Gulik continue adventures of Judge Dee and his companions. An evil Taoist monastery, seemingly supernatural events; overgrown topiary maze that hides strange crimes. Set in 7th-century China. 27 illustrations. 328pp. 5⅜ × 8½.
23502-5 Pa. $6.95

CELEBRATED CASES OF JUDGE DEE (DEE GOONG AN), translated by Robert Van Gulik. Authentic 18th-century Chinese detective novel; Dee and associates solve three interlocked cases. Led to Van Gulik's own stories with same characters. Extensive introduction. 9 illustrations. 237pp. 5⅜ × 8½.
23337-5 Pa. $5.95

Prices subject to change without notice.

Available at your book dealer or write for free catalog to Dept. GI, Dover Publications, Inc., 31 East 2nd St., Mineola, N.Y. 11501. Dover publishes more than 400 books each year on science, elementary and advanced mathematics, biology, music, art, literary history, social sciences and other areas.